ANTITRUST

after

Microsoft

The Obsolescence of Antitrust
in the Digital Era

By David B. Kopel

Foreword by Joseph Bast

THE HEARTLAND INSTITUTE

Chicago, Illinois

Published in the United States of America 2001 by
The Heartland Institute
19 South LaSalle Street, Suite 903
Chicago, Illinois 60603

Library of Congress Cataloging-in-Publication Data

Kopel, David B.
    Antitrust after Microsoft: The obsolescence of antitrust in the digital era / by David B.
Kopel ; foreword by Joseph Bast.
      p. cm.
    Includes bibliographical references and index.
    ISBN 0-9632027-5-8
        1. Computer software industry--Law and legislation--United States. 2. Antitrust law--
United States. 3. Restraint of trade--United States. 4. Microsoft Corporation. I. Title.

    KF1890.C6 K67 2001
    343.73'0721--dc21

                                                                                2001016629

ISBN 0-9632027-5-8

Manufactured in the United States of America

Dedicated to the

memory of

Mamie Toll

Table of Contents

Foreword

I n June 1999, The Heartland Institute launched its Center on the Digital Economy, a project that brings together experts from academia, industry, and think tanks to produce seminal research, publicize and popularize the work of other experts, and host events directed at policymakers and opinion leaders. This is the first book produced as a result of that effort.

THE NEW ECONOMY

Virtually all industries and all institutions are being affected by revolutionary advances in computer and telecommunications technologies. The Digital Economy is characterized by rapid change, huge economies of scale, lower production and sales costs, and rising productivity. The consequences extend from agriculture and accounting to how election campaigns are managed and when parts are delivered to automobile plants.

The arrival of the Digital Economy raises a major public policy question: Do the sweeping social and economic changes caused by the Digital Economy require similarly dramatic changes in public policy?

Answering "yes" to this question opens the door to a plethora of additional questions: Can government change quickly enough to keep pace with the new requirements and rules of business organization? If it cannot, must we reconsider its very role as regulator of business behavior in the information technology (IT) sector? And if government cannot effectively and constructively regulate the IT sector, how can it regulate other sectors of the economy transformed by the digital revolution?

We agree at the outset with the following recommendations of the Secretariat on Electronic Commerce at the U.S. Department of Commerce, as presented in its 1999 report, "The Emerging Digital Economy":

1. Governments must allow electronic commerce to grow up in an environment driven by markets, not burdened with extensive regulation, taxation, or censorship. While government actions will not stop the growth of electronic commerce, if they are too intrusive, progress can be substantially impeded.

2. Where possible, rules for the Internet and electronic commerce should result from private collective action, not government regulation.

3. Governments do have a role to play in supporting the creation of a predictable legal environment globally for doing business on the Internet, but must exercise this role in a non-bureaucratic fashion.

4. Greater competition in telecommunications and broadcast industries should be encouraged so that high-bandwidth services are brought to homes and offices around the world and so that the new converged marketplace of broadcast, telephony, and the Internet operate based on laws of competition and consumer choice rather than those of government regulation.

5. There should be no discriminatory taxation against Internet commerce.

6. The Internet should function as a seamless global marketplace with no artificial barriers erected by governments.

To the Secretariat's list we add the following two principles:

7. Protection of private property rights is an essential condition for effective planning and the long-term growth of the Digital Economy.

8. Effective public policy advocacy and education are required to overcome opposition to change by special interest groups if the public is to benefit from the many opportunities and efficiencies made possible by the digital revolution.

David B. Kopel and others writing for the Center on the Digital Economy argue that market choices, not politics, should dictate the growth and organization of the Digital Economy. Their argument is persuasive. Competition, property rights, and consumer choice appear to be more reliable means to ensure efficiency and consumer benefits in the twenty-first century than bureaucracy and top-down command-and-control regulation.

THE MICROSOFT CASE

The U.S. Department of Justice's lawsuit against Microsoft Corporation, filed in 1998, makes for an interesting case study of the role of regulation in the Digital Economy.

In some respects it is a difficult way to approach the debate about the proper role of government. Even many economists would argue that private-sector monopolies may theoretically justify government intervention. David B. Kopel contends, however, that the pace of change is now so great in the IT industry, and is about to become almost as fast in other parts of the economy, that the rationale even for antitrust law has crumbled.

There is a sort of poetic justice in the way Kopel uses the Microsoft case to make the two sides in the dispute trade places. Here, antitrust law and its defenders are on trial. They are guilty of collusion, of indifference to the interests of consumers, and ultimately of threatening force to preserve the status quo against new companies, new products, and new ideas. Of course, these are among the sins of which Microsoft stands accused.

Kopel's work is important because defenders of individual liberty and free enterprise must make their views known in the debate over government's role in the Digital Economy. Without them, the debate will be dominated by those most heavily invested in the services and technologies of the past. These latter interest groups can use their political clout and access to opinion leaders to slow and skew the processes of economic change.

Choosing to sit out the debate on the grounds that Microsoft is "big enough to defend itself," or that this controversy affects "only" the IT industry, is foolhardy. All of us, no matter what our occupation or interests, have a stake in the outcome.

Joseph L. Bast
President
The Heartland Institute

Chicago, January 1, 2001

Introduction

T he antitrust lawsuit brought against Microsoft Corporation in May 1998 by the U.S. Department of Justice and 19 state attorneys general, whose appeal was pending as this book was written, marks the end of an era of antitrust law theory, legislation, and action. Regardless of which side wins, antitrust policy in the twenty-first century will be far different from what it was in the nineteenth, when the laws were first written, or in the twentieth, when it was put to use in a series of landmark cases that define the terms of the debate today.

TIME AND TECHNOLOGY

A principal theme of this book is that technology profoundly affects industries and markets, and that unless laws keep up with the effects of technology, they will produce disappointing results. It is worth a few minutes, therefore, to quickly review the notion of "Internet Time."

The technologies of the Industrial Revolution—the internal combustion engine, electricity, airplanes, and so much more—changed our concepts of time. Tasks that once consumed hours now required just minutes. Trips that took days

1

now lasted a few hours. The pace of daily life in areas affected by these technologies accelerated, enabling us to cram more productive activity into each minute, hour, and day. Clocks and watches, "instruments to measure the flight of time in a culture conscious of both time and movement,"[1] first became pervasively popular during the 1890s. Those parts of our lives less affected by the new technologies—e.g., gardening, reading a good book, parenting— continued at their slower pace, though even they of course were not entirely unaffected by changing technology.

The impact of technology on civilization was to create in people's minds two different senses of time, one appropriate to activities involving movement, commerce, and production, the other more appropriate to stillness, recreation, and leisure. Whether the split was a good thing or a bad thing we can leave to philosophers and historians.

The technology of the Industrial Revolution did away with local methods of timekeeping. If a person looked up at the sky in 1830, he would know that noon was when the sun was on the meridian. Noon in Omaha would take place after noon in Des Moines, since Omaha is further west. This system of keeping time worked well for many years, but the heightened pace of economic and social activity and the increased scale of commerce made possible by the Industrial Revolution soon exposed the old system's flaws.

In 1883, American railroad companies solved the problem by developing "railroad time," eventually dividing the country into four time zones.[2] Now, noon would take place at the same moment in Chicago, Des Moines, and Omaha—all in the same time zone—even though the sun would not be exactly on the meridian at noon in any of the three cities. This made coordinating railroad schedules much easier. In 1918, a generation after railroad time was adopted by the private sector, Congress formally adopted "Standard Time."

THE DIGITAL ECONOMY

Today, clocks are still set to Standard Time or to the variant called Daylight Savings Time.[3] But the technologies of the Industrial Revolution have themselves been superceded by a new set of technologies involving data

---

[1]Howard Mumford Jones, *The Age of Energy: Varieties of American Experience, 1865-1915* (New York, NY: Viking Press, 1971), page 150.

[2]England's Great Western Railway was the first to create its own time, in November 1840.

[3]Except in Arizona, Hawaii, 77 counties of Indiana, and a few other places.

processing, transmission, and storage: the Digital Revolution. Today the part of the national economy that manufactures, delivers, or relies on information technology (IT) is changing about four times as fast as the rest of the economy.[4] A rule of thumb, then, is that three months of this so-called "Internet Time" equals one year of Standard Time.

Things really do happen faster on Internet Time.

Consider one benchmark of technological diffusion, the time required for a product to reach 25 percent of consumers. That interval has steadily shrunk over time.

It took half a century from the day controllable electricity was invented for 25 percent of American homes to have electricity. There was a 50-year lag between the invention of the automobile and the day 25 percent of American households owned a car. Airplane travel also took half a century to reach the 25 percent penetration level.

Radio and television were much faster, achieving 25 percent penetration in a quarter of a century. Personal computers were faster still, at 15 years, and cellular phones took only 13 years, about four times faster than the rate of diffusion of cars and airplane travel.[5]

The rapid diffusion of new technology changes how businesses operate. For example, time-to-market must be as short, and inventories must be kept as small, as possible.[6] A business operating at a speed that seems rapid in Standard Time may find it is moving much too slowly to compete with firms operating at Internet Time. Barry Diller, president of USA Networks, referring to lessons learned from his failed Home Shopping Network Internet Project, warns others not to fund systems that will take more than nine months to complete, since otherwise they will be obsolete before they are done.[7]

Nine months? Just a decade ago in Standard Time it would have been unthinkable to suppose that a nationally marketed product or service could move from idea to sales in so little time. Yet the business press is full of

---

[4]Stacy Lawrence, "Internet in Media Time," *The Industry Standard*, May 8, 2000, page 208. Others suggest Internet Time may be even faster: one calendar year equaling seven Internet years. See Dori Jones Yang, "Laying in for the Long Siege," *U.S. News & World Report*, April 17, 2000, page 42.

[5]Robert E. Litan and William A. Niskanen, *Going Digital* (Washington, DC: Brookings Institution and Cato Institute, 1998), page 32. Household television ownership blossomed from just under 10 percent in 1950 to 65 percent in 1955. Internet access expansion has not been quite that fast, growing from 10 percent of households in 1995 to about half in 2000.

[6]See Bill Gates, *Business @ the Speed of Thought* (New York, NY: Warner Books, 1999); Philip Evans and Thomas S. Wurster, *Blown to Bits* (Boston, MA: Harvard Business School Press, 2000); and Carl Shapiro and Hal R. Varian, *Information Rules* (Boston, MA: Harvard Business School Press, 1999).

[7]John McCormick, "Lessons for Learning," *Inter@ctive Week*, April 17, 2000, page 46.

stories of successful (and unsuccessful) business start-ups, new product lines, and major corporate reorganizations taking place on timelines this short or shorter. Plainly, Internet Time has profoundly changed the rules for businesses in the IT industry, and increasingly for businesses in the Old Economy.

TIME AND REGULATION

Governments are usually less able than private businesses to keep pace with technological change. The reasons have been described at length by many prominent scholars and deep thinkers over the years,[8] but they come down to issues of structure, information, and incentives.

Government agencies are often deliberately structured to slow down decision-making to allow for input from a variety of stakeholders and elected officials or to limit the power of any one agency or branch of government. What is commonly deplored as "red tape" is actually the way a bureaucracy attempts to ensure accountability.

Because government agencies seldom rely on markets to acquire income or "sell" their services, they have little reliable information about consumer preferences or how competitors deliver similar products or services more efficiently. Whereas private-sector firms can use their competitors' methods and prices as benchmarks for their own decisions, governments are usually monopolists in their geographic area.

Finally, the leaders of even a streamlined government agency relying on market signals to make important decisions will have few incentives to respond promptly and correctly to those signals. Job security, higher salary and status, and political advantage in the public sector all are more likely to come from expanding the size of one's budget and staff than from contracting them.

Government indeed is lagging behind the pace of technological change. The U.S. Department of Commerce, for example, is scheduled to publish its latest data on electronic commerce—containing information from 1998 and 1999—in 2001.[9] Government's failure to manage technology is contributing to major

---

[8]Thomas Sowell, *Knowledge and Decisions* (New York, NY: Basic Books, Inc., 1980); James M. Buchanan, *Public Finance in Democratic Process* (Chapel Hill, NC: The University of North Carolina Press, 1987 [1967]); James Q. Wilson, *On Bureaucracy: What Governments Do and Why They Do It* (New York, NY: Basic Books, 1989).

[9] Louis Trager, "Government E-Commerce Data to Come Out at a Crawl," *Inter@ctive Week*, March 13, 2000, page 22.

congestion and safety problems at the nation's airports.[10]

When Government Time clashes with Internet Time, the risk of mistakes is high. A report issued by The Brookings Institution and Cato Institute explains:

> The constantly changing nature of digital technologies means that government intervention in the digital field runs high risks not only of being premature—a technological solution may be quickly developed that is far more effective than any regulatory edict—but also of frustrating further innovation if the intervention is misplaced, or falls victim to the law of unintended consequences (as so many government interventions do).[11]

The Sherman Act was passed about a decade after Alexander Graham Bell invented the telephone. Yet Joel Klein, the Antitrust Division chief who started the Microsoft case, argues antitrust is perfect for the age of the Digital Economy: "Given the speed of today's economy, antitrust is going to become the only legitimate form of government intervention."[12]

Is Mr. Klein right? There is, as I attempt to show in what follows, plenty of room for doubt.

We begin, in Chapters One and Two, by examining how things have changed in the two-and-a-half years of Standard Time that have passed since the Department of Justice sued Microsoft in May 1998. During that time, software once thought superior has become obsolete, while software given little chance of success is winning. Technologies thought to be state-of-the-art have been superceded by hardware that is faster, smarter, and cheaper.

The competitive environment also has been transformed. Competitors who once complained of Microsoft's market power have now merged with other competitors, becoming behemoths themselves. Chapter Two examines the new competition to Microsoft's core business, the personal computer operating system, from Linux and Apple, and also describes how the center of gravity for computing is shifting away from the PC and onto such devices as Internet appliances, personal digital assistants, Web-enabled telephones, and other tools.

This mercurial situation compels us to ask several questions:

What are the effects of these changes on the immediate case concerning

---

[10]Robert W. Poole Jr., *Instead of Regulation: Alternatives to Federal Regulatory Agencies* (Lexington, MA: Lexington Books, 1982).

[11]Robert E. Litan and William A. Niskanen, *Going Digital*, *supra* note 5, page 53.

[12]"Klein: Put Trust in Antitrust," *Wired News*, May 18, 2000.

Microsoft? Are the original charges still meaningful? Is the proposed remedy still to anyone's benefit?

What do these changes mean for antitrust enforcement generally? Can antitrust laws be intelligently imposed on *any* companies in the Digital Economy?

If antitrust law is obsolete, what accounts for its continued use against companies such as Microsoft?

Chapter Three discusses whether Microsoft's large market share in PC operating systems and productivity suites is tantamount to a monopoly. Chapter Four analyzes various complaints raised about Microsoft's conduct in marketing the Windows operating system, while Chapter Five looks at complaints about the marketing of the Internet Explorer Web browser.

Chapter Six addresses the issue of consumer harm and the appropriateness of the various remedies, including breakup, imposed by the trial judge. Chapter Seven examines the history of transportation regulation and then some of the most famous antitrust cases in history in an effort to uncover the myths and legends that often substitute for factual knowledge in the debate over antitrust law. Chapter Seven also reviews some of the statements made by Microsoft's critics early in the Microsoft case to see how well they have stood the test of time.

Chapter Eight looks at the role politics has played in shaping antitrust regulation and enforcement in general, and specifically in the case involving Microsoft. Chapter Nine summarizes some of the earlier findings of the book and states some conclusions.

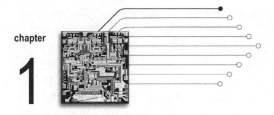

1

New Technologies

During the two-and-a-half years of Standard Time that have passed since the Microsoft case began, as much technological change has occurred in the information technology (IT) industry as was experienced by the rest of the economy in the past decade. During this decade of Internet Time, new technologies evolved more rapidly than even the most prescient techno-visionaries predicted. Internet connections are now hundreds of times faster than those commonly in use when the Microsoft trial began. Hard drive disk storage capacities have been doubling every nine months, and the cost of personal computers has been plunging. With Internet access now available free from several national vendors, the decade-old fear that Microsoft would monopolize the Internet seems far-fetched. These developments and others discussed below cast serious doubt upon the ability of government to apply traditional antitrust remedies to the ever-changing technological marketplace.

FROM MAINFRAME TO LAPTOP

To understand the technological changes that have occurred since 1998, our story must start some 30 years earlier, in 1969. That year, the Department of Justice brought an antitrust case against IBM, complaining the company had integrated too many improvements into its computers, allegedly preventing development of strong separate markets for those add-ons. At the time, IBM had 78 percent (by revenue) of the market for electronic data processing.[1] The market consisted of mainframe computers, the only kind of computers that existed at the time.

IBM had specialized in selling mainframes to central accounting or data processing departments. A group of new competitors, however, recognized that many people in business did not want to be dependent on "the" computer in a central office; they wanted their department to have its own computer, which they could use without having to wait in line for the company's only computer to become available. Thus, the minicomputer came into its own, from companies such as Digital Equipment, Data General, Prime, Wang, and Nixdorf. IBM eventually introduced its own minicomputers, but it never established the dominant position it had enjoyed for mainframes. IBM saw its market share plunge to 33 percent by 1972.[2]

The minicomputer companies that prospered in the 1970s and early 1980s were devastated in the late 1980s by the rise of the personal computer. PCs further distributed computing power by allowing ordinary workers to have computers on their desktops. The leading PC makers were not the companies that led the minicomputer market; rather, they were Apple, IBM, Commodore, and Tandy.[3] The leading desktop PC manufacturers, in turn, were soon playing second fiddle to the manufacturers of portable computers and eventually laptops, for which the leading companies became Toshiba, Sharp, and Zenith.

When Microsoft entered the computer business in 1975, the paradigm was still low-volume/high-cost: Sell a small volume of the product, but sell it to affluent buyers who will pay top dollar. The extreme version of this model might be the mainframe computer, with only a few dozen customers. But the general version of the model represented the way many successful computer

---

[1]Dominick T. Armentano, *Antitrust: The Case for Repeal* (Auburn, AL: Ludwig von Mises Institute, 1999 (second edition)), page 15.

[2]Clayton M. Christensen, *The Innovator's Dilemma: When New Technologies Cause Great Firms to Fail* (Boston, MA: Harvard Business School Press, 1997), pages 108-109.

[3] Dominick T. Armentano, *Antitrust: The Case for Repeal, supra* note 1.

companies (such as Apple) operated for many years.

Other companies tried to take on the established giants with an opposite strategy of high-volume/low-cost. Commodore was one example, with its PET computers designed to put computing power into the hands of college science majors who loved to write computer programs, but hated waiting around at the university computer center for terminal time.

One very important reason for the spread of personal computing since 1989 has been the availability of an ever-improving graphical interface for inexpensive computers. Apple had introduced a great interface years before, but the software and hardware were expensive. It was the Windows interface that made personal computing, and the Internet, available to tens of millions of people who once thought they could never learn to use a computer.

No company in the Digital Economy has pursued high-volume/low-cost for a longer time and more aggressively than has Microsoft. The Microsoft model was far more prevalent among computer businesses in the year 2001 than it was in the year 1980. Bill Gates did not create this revolution single-handedly, but he must rank as one of the most important of its founding fathers.

With this background in mind, let's look at more recent technological innovations since 1998. They fall into four categories: increasing speed, falling cost, new media, and e-commerce.

FAST, FASTER, INSTANT

For the last quarter-century, Moore's Law has governed the advance of computer technology. Gordon Moore, the founder of Intel, observed that microprocessor performance doubles approximately every 18 months. But in telecommunications, Moore's Law is proving too modest, as optical technology triples or quadruples performance every year. The leading cause is the fantastic advance in communications fibers. The national telephone system in 2001 will have *80 times* the capacity it had in 1996.[4]

In the "old" days (say, the 1980s), communications fibers (such as a telephone company's trunk lines) conveyed data by sending streams of electrical signals (electrons) down a copper line. Then copper lines were replaced by fiber-optic cables, in which laser-created light signals (photons) are sent through glass tubing. With both copper and early fiber-optics, a single line could carry only a single stream of data at a time. But now, scientists have found a way to make a single fiber-optic glass cable carry many signals at once: The laser sends

---

[4]Rachael King, "Too Much Long Distance," *Fortune*, March 15, 1999, page 107.

different data streams in different colors of light. This "Dense Wavelength Division Multiplexing" allows data carriers to transmit hundreds of times more capacity, without laying a single new cable.[5]

Fiber-optics move data at high speed across the cables that make up the backbone of the Internet, but they do not move data "the last mile" into a customer's home. When the Microsoft trial began, home computer connections to the Internet were made almost exclusively via dial-up telephone lines whose maximum connection speed was 56 kbps. Today, cable television companies such as AOL/Time Warner, AT&T, and many others are installing high-speed cable modems that bring the Internet into homes via upgraded cable television lines. These connections are much faster than the ordinary 56k dial-up connection.

Spurred by the competition from the cable companies, telephone companies are aggressively introducing high-speed Digital Subscriber Lines ("DSL"). DSL connections are at least four times as fast as "old-fashioned" dial-up modems, and can be dozens of times faster. Even the old-fashioned modems are two to four times faster than the modems that were common when Windows 95 was introduced, and over 20 times faster than the modems typical when Windows 3.0 was brought to market in 1989.

Small satellite dishes are increasingly used for high-speed Internet access as well as multi-channel television program distribution. In March 2000, a company called TeraBeam announced what George Gilder pronounced to be "the most disruptive and most redemptive technology in all communications. I have been looking for such a company for a decade."[6] TeraBeam creates a point-to-point laser communications network. The TeraBeam box sits in the window of a home or office, costs about $150 to make, and connects to the Internet at a speed of up to two gigabits per second, 80 times faster than most high-speed DSL and cable modem connections and hundreds of times faster than dial-up modems.

When the Microsoft trial began, techno-visionaries were forecasting that ultra-fast Internet connections to the home would not be deployed until around 2020, when fiber-optic lines would be laid into each home. Now, ultra-fast connections are imminent. Soon, the connection between a keyboard and a Web server will be as fast as between a keyboard and a home computer.

The movement of applications off the personal computer and onto the Internet (discussed below) will be greatly facilitated by the proliferation of high-

---

[5] Joe McGarvey, "Net Gear Breaks Moore's Law," *Inter@ctive Week*, April 17, 2000, page 74.

[6] "Laser Guided," *The Economist*, March 25, 2000.

speed Internet connections. A 56k connection may not support intensive word processing over the Internet, but a 1mb connection can.

The main limitation in the deployment of such broadband technologies has not been technical, but a lack of compelling content. As of mid-2000, at least 70 million homes had access to high-speed broadband from either cable or DSL, and some had access to both. Yet only a few million homes have chosen to subscribe. The reason is that even though broadband may cost only $10-$20 per month more than dial-up Internet, most users have not found a compelling reason to pay more for high-speed access. Email is fast enough already, and a Web page that loads in one second instead of five may not be worth $15 a month.

The future growth of broadband, and hence the growth of the Internet as an alternative applications platform, depends on companies that can create the video and other content that makes broadband appealing. These companies include TimeWarner (now part of AOL/Netscape), which is both a content creator and the owner of many cable television lines. AOL, meanwhile, has cut preferential placement deals with many telephone companies that supply DSL. In April 2000, AOL began providing streaming video and audio through high-speed Internet connections.[7]

Accommodating the enormous amount of data required for audio and video transmissions requires larger hard drive capacities, and here again we see major technological breakthroughs. Hard drive capacity is doubling every nine months, moving twice as fast as Moore's Law. An ordinary PC now comes with a dozen or more gigabytes of storage, and power users are buying 180gb drives. In 2003, terabyte-sized disks (able to store 400 full-length movies) will be available.[8]

This massive storage capacity may help PCs stave off the competition from handheld devices such as personal digital assistants and the like (more on them below). On the other hand, storage advances will also help the small devices. IBM has announced a disk drive smaller than a matchbook that stores a gigabyte (20,000 pages of text).[9] This drive could give a digital phone or Palm Pilot more storage capacity than most desktop computers had when Windows 95 was introduced.

---

[7]"AOL to Offer Streaming Video," *Chicago Sun-Times*, April 5, 2000.

[8]Dori Jones Yang, "Leaving Moore's Law in the Dust," *U.S. News & World Report*, July 10, 2000, page 37.

[9]*Ibid.*

CHEAP, CHEAPER, FREE

Since 1971, the cost of computing has fallen fantastically. In 1970, one megahertz of processing power cost $7,600.82. By 1999, the cost was 17 cents. In 1970, one megabit of storage cost $5,256.90; in 1999, 17 cents. In 1970, the cost of sending one trillion bits was $150,000; in 1999, 12 cents.[10]

PC costs have plunged from the $1,300-$1,700 level down to $399 for entry-level products from companies like eMachines. These machines are much faster than a high-quality business machine from a few years ago. Promotions come and go for free PCs in exchange for three-year Internet service contracts costing $20 to $25 per month. Home computers are also being distributed for free or at steeply discounted prices by major employers such as Ford Motor Co., Intel Corp., Delta Air Lines, and American Airlines.[11]

These developments bring to mind an internal Microsoft memo from 1995: "My nightmare scenario is that the Web grows into a rich application platform in an operating system-neutral way" and a computer maker brings out a $500 machine capable of surfing the Internet. Then, "say good-bye to Windows."[12] That nightmare has come true, as detailed below in the discussion of Web applications.

More and more digital or communication services are becoming available for free. One can get free Web-based faxing from such companies as Fax4Free and eFax, free email, free calendar programs, free fantasy sports, and scores of other free programs that weren't free in 1998 or hadn't even been invented then.

There is free Web hosting from Yahoo!, Juno, and many others. Free Internet access is offered by such Internet Service Providers (ISPs) as Netzero (3 million members), 1stUp.com, and K-Mart's Blue Light.[13] A decade ago in Internet Time, when the Microsoft case began, there were predictions that Microsoft would monopolize the browser market and then achieve dominance as an ISP, charging consumers and businesses high prices for Internet

---

[10] Federal Reserve Bank of Dallas, *The New Paradigm* (1999 Annual Report), page 8. *The New Paradigm* offers an excellent summary of how computers are transforming the economy.

[11] See, for example, "Intel Home PC Program," www.intel.com/jobs/bencomp/.

[12] John R. Wilke and Keith Perine, "Final Government Witness Testifies Against Microsoft in Antitrust Trial," *Wall Street Journal*, January 6, 1999; Franklin M. Fisher and Daniel L. Rubinfeld, "*United States v. Microsoft*: An Economic Analysis," in David S. Evans, Franklin M. Fisher, Daniel L. Rubinfeld, and Richard L. Schmalensee, *Did Microsoft Harm Consumers? Two Opposing Views* (Washington, DC: AEI-Brookings Joint Center for Regulatory Studies, 2000), page 111, note 20.

[13] Jason Krause, "Free Access Spreads Its Wings," *The Industry Standard*, May 8, 2000, page 67; Max Smetannikov, "Big Brands Crashing Party," *Inter@ctive Week*, February 7, 2000, page 52.

connections. Today, Microsoft is a respectable but far from top-ranking ISP, and the risk of monopoly pricing in a market where competitors give their products away for free seems small indeed.

NEW MEDIA AND OLD MEDIA

In the first seven days of 1999, AOL enrolled as many new customers (180,000) as it did in its first seven years.[14] Time spent online continues to increase very rapidly. It is predicted that by 2003, Americans will spend more time online than they do reading cellulose newspapers.[15] Spending on Internet advertising in 2000 is 23 times the level of 1995; advertising growth on the Internet far exceeds the growth rates from the early days of broadcast television, cable television, or radio.[16]

Nevertheless, as *Slate*, DrKoop.com, and other content-based Web sites found out the hard way, charging for news and commentary is difficult, even when it is of high quality and on important or popular topics. Companies that have succeeded in making money by charging online users are those that traffic in difficult-to-find financial analysis, such as Bloomberg News and Dow Jones, publisher of the *Wall Street Journal*. Business-to-business e-newsletters linked to services for e-commerce show promise, and pornography continues to be a multi-billion-dollar industry on the Web.

The Web model for non-specialized and non-pornographic information seems to be "information is free," with advertisers expected to carry the freight. The collapse of Internet stocks in mid-2000 was driven in part by investors coming to realize that advertising could not generate enough revenue to cover the operating costs of many dot-coms and still generate profits.

While the Web model is in flux, the notion of "free information" is starting to affect even the old media. For example, every day in Philadelphia, consumers pick up 150,000 copies of the free *Metro* newspaper. *Metro*'s Swedish publisher, Veronis Suhler, is launching free daily print newspapers in 60 cities worldwide. Managing Director Robert J. Broadwater explains how the new media changed the old media: "In the past there's been a stigma associated with free circulation media. But that stigma is largely eroding. . . . On the Web,

---

[14]Nelson D. Schwartz, "The Tech Boom Will Keep on Rocking," *Fortune*, February 15, 1999, page 69.

[15]Stacy Lawrence, "Internet in Media Time," *The Industry Standard*, May 8, 2000, page 208.

[16]*Ibid.*

you're training a whole generation of people that intellectual property is free."[17]

The evolution of new media and new technologies does not mean the older ones are going to whither away—if they are smart and adaptable. Many radio stations are doing better than ever. One reason is that the Telecommunications Act of 1996 allows greater consolidation of radio station ownership, which in turn allows radio to offer a national buy to advertisers for the first time; potential radio advertisers no longer have to contact hundreds of stations separately. Radio stations are now broadcasting on the Internet, reaching audiences far beyond the geographical boundaries of their signal strength. Also, advertising by Internet companies, such as Yahoo! or Priceline.com, is focused on building brand-name identification, and is therefore perfect for radio.

It would have seemed impossible 10 years ago, but today the entire *Encyclopedia Britannica* is available for free on the Internet at www.britannica.com. One reason for *Britannica*'s radical move to free Internet distribution was competition from CD-ROM encyclopedias, particularly Microsoft Encarta. Indeed, Microsoft was one of the first companies to realize the potential of CD-ROM. According to Chris E. Hall and Robert E. Hall, "the company was a pioneer in distributing content on CD-ROMs and transformed the encyclopedia market in the process, bringing the price of encyclopedias down by a factor of 10."[18] The "Microsoft Bookshelf" CD put a dictionary, spell-checker, thesaurus, and small encyclopedia on a compact disk for the first time.

Notably, the move to the Web plays to *Britannica*'s strength compared with other Web sites. On the Internet, where so much information is available, credibility and reliability are very valuable commodities, and *Britannica* has both.[19]

E-COMMERCE

Time magazine named Amazon.com founder and CEO Jeff Bezos Man of the Year for 1999. Bezos not only revolutionized the book business, but he also created a new model of e-commerce with such innovations as one-click buying.

Even as the Department of Justice was explaining to the trial judge how

---

[17]Marci McDonald, "All the News that Fits—and It's Free," *U.S. News & World Report*, February 7, 2000, page 40.

[18]Chris E. Hall and Robert E. Hall, *National Policy on Microsoft: A Neutral Perspective* (version 2.0, 1999), page 64, www.NetEcon.com.

[19]James Coates and Darnell Little, "Thirst for Knowledge Drowns Site," *Chicago Tribune*, October 27, 1999.

Microsoft was stifling innovation, Bezos became the number-one Web entrepreneur while having absolutely nothing to do with Microsoft. During the first two calendar years consumed by the Microsoft case, Amazon.com's gross sales rose more than ten-fold.[20] Amazon.com's Web site does not use any Microsoft software. The Amazon.com Web pages are not optimized for Microsoft's Internet Explorer Web browser. Amazon has never entered into a reciprocal promotional arrangement with Microsoft—such as promoting Internet Explorer in exchange for links from the Microsoft desktop or Web portal. Amazon's success casts doubt on the warnings at the beginning of the Microsoft case that Microsoft was developing a "chokehold on the Internet"—especially on electronic commerce.

While Amazon.com never had a business relationship with Microsoft, its business plan nevertheless depends on Microsoft's success. Microsoft's strategies of mass production, mass distribution, and low prices expanded the market for PCs far beyond its previous base of businesses, hobbyists, and the wealthy. The millions of households that bought PCs for the first time in the 1990s are now Amazon.com's customers.

Books are hardly the only product being transformed by the Internet. Cars are another. Ford is one of the many Old Economy companies taking advantage of popular private ownership of PCs and the ubiquitous Windows operating system to increase efficiency, profits, and customer satisfaction. Ford has begun building cars based on specific customer orders, so that each day's production depends on the previous day's orders. The process helps Ford give its customers the cars they really want and makes Ford's orders to parts suppliers more in tune with Ford's needs.[21]

The changes at Ford are part of a more general evolution of American business, made possible by the digital revolution, toward "mass customization": manufacturing what people specifically ask for, rather than manufacturing a standard product and only then trying to get people to buy it.

E-commerce is dramatically lowering the cost of business-to-business ("B2B") commerce as Internet auctions, reverse auctions,[22] and industry exchanges using infomediaries[23] bring buyers and sellers together and expedite

---

[20]Dori Jones Yang, "Laying in for the Long Siege," *U.S. News & World Report*, April 17, 2000, page 42.

[21]William J. Holstein, "The Dot.com within Ford," *U.S. News & World Report*, February 7, 2000, page 34.

[22] Shawn Tully, "The B2B Tool that Really *Is* Changing the World," *Fortune*, March 20, 2000, page 132. In a reverse auction the buyer starts by posting a price he will pay for something (*e.g.*, 100,000 widgets). During the auction period, potential sellers bid lower and lower prices at which they will supply the item.

[23]People who match buyers and sellers who do not know each other.

the ordering and contracting processes. The spread of computers is widely acknowledged to be the major contributor to productivity gains during the second half of the 1990s.[24] Output per hour grew 0.7 percent annually from 1992 to 1995, and then at quadruple that rate, 2.8 percent annually, from 1996 to 1999.

BRIEFLY STATED . . .

The vast changes in technology that have taken place in just the past two-and-a-half years defy brief description. For example, we haven't even touched on the fields of biotechnology, robotics, or nanotechnology, each characterized by technological advances during a single year, 2000, that have tremendous consequences for businesses in a score of industries.

The phenomenal increases in the power of computers and speed of data transmission are making possible new forms of content and services undreamt of just a few years ago. Business practices have changed to keep pace with technology. Products that were at the core of the Microsoft case when it was filed in 1998 have disappeared, changed dramatically, been superceded by others, or been sold or merged with others. The result is a product landscape that would be almost unrecognizable to a juror or jurist studying Microsoft in 1998.

Technological change *per se* does not mean the Microsoft case ought to be dropped. It certainly does not mean Microsoft is innocent of the illegal business practices it is charged with. Those are separate and important matters taken up below. What *is* clear, though, is that Microsoft's actions have not stopped or even slowed the rate of technological innovation and change that has occurred since the suit was filed. Indeed, Microsoft products continue to play a major role in making much of that innovation possible.

The proliferation of new products and falling prices makes it difficult to defend the assertion that consumers were harmed during the 1990s by Microsoft's alleged monopolistic conduct. A much more likely explanation of what happened during the 1990s is that capital gravitated to the IT industry *because* it was lightly regulated by government and therefore able to innovate and grow rapidly. This characterization requires that we move beyond mere technological change, to investigate the companies behind the products and the tactics they used.

---

[24]N. Gregory Mankiw, "D.C., Stay Out of the New Economy," *Fortune*, May 15, 2000, page 70.

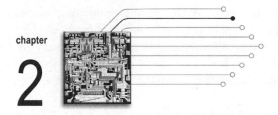

New Competitors

A major premise of the May 1998 antitrust action was that Microsoft faced no competition in the operating systems market for personal computers. In the decade (Internet Time) since then, however, Apple Computers has staged an impressive comeback and the Linux operating system has enjoyed explosive growth, particularly in the business environment.

The computer world is undergoing a paradigm shift not unlike the change from the Copernican to the Galilean view of the universe. With every passing year of Internet Time, the computing universe grows less centered on the desktop personal computer. Computing applications are now appearing on a wide variety of non-desktop computers, including handheld devices such as the Palm Pilot, digital phones that can access and use the Internet, and gaming machines that run computer applications. Even for personal computers, applications are beginning to migrate off the PC in two directions: onto the microprocessor chip and onto the Internet. Today, the idea that Microsoft will be able to maintain its commanding share of the market for operating systems for computers used by individuals looks much less tenable than it did in May 1998.

APPLE'S COMEBACK

In the early 1980s, Apple Computers was on top of the computing world. Although Xerox had developed the graphical interface, Apple improved it and brought it to the mass personal computer market. The intuitive and easy-to-understand interface made Apple an ideal first computer for millions of consumers. In the mid-1980s Apple's founder and CEO Steve Jobs epitomized the successful computer entrepreneur.

If a consumer wanted to use the well-regarded Apple operating system, he had exactly one choice of hardware manufacturer: Apple. As a vertically integrated software and hardware manufacturer, Apple tied its products together inextricably. This is the same business strategy followed today by companies, such as Sun Microsystems, that sell computers for large business networks. The Sun Solaris operating system runs only on Sun computers. Apple, like Sun, did allow third-party vendors (Independent Software Vendors, or ISVs) to make applications programs for Apple computers running Apple OS. During the 1980s, a little-known company named Microsoft earned much of its revenue from a word processing program it wrote for Apple computers. Even so, a great deal of the leading applications software for the Apple hardware/OS was made by Apple itself.

Apple followed the high-price/low-volume strategy, maximizing short-term revenues from the OS/hardware combination. Fortunately for Apple, however, this high-priced "bundling" of hardware and OS was ignored by the Reagan Department of Justice, which took a relatively relaxed view of antitrust laws and which (like most of the rest of the federal government) was not paying much attention to personal computers.

Unfortunately for Apple, its monopoly-type business strategy caused the company serious problems in the long run. Because Apple's prices were so high, there was an opportunity for other companies to underprice it. Many computers of the day were not powerful enough to run Apple's graphical interface (not that Apple would have sold the manufacturers a license anyway), but those computers could run the command-line Disk Operating System (DOS) from IBM and Microsoft. DOS made fewer demands on the computer and thus was well-suited to less-powerful computers, though it made more demands on the user, who had to type short commands to start a program or move files, rather than simply pointing and clicking with a mouse in the Apple OS. It turned out there were millions of buyers—in fact, the large majority of PC buyers—who would put up with a more challenging OS interface in exchange for saving $500-$1,000 on the computer. DOS-based applications software was also cheaper.

Computers running DOS had another advantage. When Apple brought out improved versions of its OS, it did not make the new OS backwards-compatible. A computer with the new Apple OS would not run software written for the previous Apple OS. The absence of backwards-compatibility made creation of the new OS less expensive and made the new OS work better. But it also alienated Apple customers who had paid hundreds of dollars for software that could never be used on a new Apple computer. Persons who were considering whether to buy an Apple or DOS computer noticed (or heard from friends) that buying an Apple today would require buying an entirely new Apple to upgrade a few years later and then having to spend even more money to replace existing applications programs. By contrast, each version of DOS was compatible with applications software from older versions. If one owned a program written for DOS 2.0, it would run on DOS 3.0.

In the late 1980s and early 1990s, advances in computer hardware made it possible for new computers in the $1,500-$2,000 price range to run a graphical interface at acceptable speeds. Graphical interfaces from Microsoft, IBM, Quarterdeck, and other companies competed for leadership, and prices for hardware and software continued to fall. Apple, meanwhile, kept its OS and hardware prices significantly higher and continued to abandon old OS owners as new OS/hardware platforms were introduced. Apple's market share fell, and by the mid-1990s, some analysts forecast the company might not survive.

A few months before the Microsoft antitrust case began, Apple had only 2.1 percent of the new-computer market.[1] Today, the Apple iMac is the best-selling personal computer in the United States. Twelve percent of iMac buyers are migrating from PCs that ran Windows.[2] And Apple is not selling just to its traditional market of schools and universities, where the offer of educational discounts had always made Apple much more competitively priced than in the general consumer market.

Clearly, Apple is doing a better job than it has in the past of competing in the PC market. Prices are lower, and Apple now allows some independent hardware manufacturers to make hardware that runs MacOS. Apple now treats its distributors better and has made various internal reforms.

There is, however, another, more fundamental change taking place.

The fast-selling iMac is marketed mainly as an Internet tool.[3] The iMac

---

[1] Susan B. Garland, "Microsoft's Defense: A Tough Sell, but Not Impossible," *Business Week*, January 18, 1999, page 44.

[2] Steven Johnson, "Apple Gains on Microsoft. No Kidding," *Wall Street Journal*, November 16, 1998.

[3] www.apple.com/imac.

customers are not, primarily, buying a personal computer to do intensive desktop applications such as advanced word processing or spreadsheet work. For such work, Apple still lags behind PCs running Windows in the performance-price ratio. Rather, the iMac is an attractive piece of furniture—curvy and available in a variety of strong colors, instead of boxy and available in beige, like most Windows-based computers. If a consumer wants a computer that is good for surfing the Internet and sending email and looks nice on the kitchen counter or in the family room, the iMac is a good choice.

It is because the Internet is such an important part of the modern computing experience that Apple had the opportunity to change the terms of the operating system competition with Microsoft it had previously lost. As Steven Johnson wrote in the *Wall Street Journal*, "The bottom line is that the Internet is indifferent to operating systems. Online standards like TCP/IP, HTML and POP are universal; Windows, MacOS and Linux are just afterthoughts."[4] The "nightmare scenario" predicted in the 1995 internal Microsoft memo of an "operating system-neutral" Web has come true.

LINUX

The MacOS and the Windows OS are both closed, proprietary systems. Their internal workings are known to the companies that sell them, but computer users and programmers cannot view the internal coding. The MacOS and Windows OS interact with the "outside world"—such as software applications—through Applications Programming Interfaces (APIs). APIs are "exposed" so that software applications developers can write code that uses the APIs. For example, if the software developer wants the software to display a dialog box, the developer tells his software application to use the API that displays dialog boxes.

The Unix operating system, by contrast, is "open source." Unix, like the MacOS and the Windows OS, lets developers use APIs, but Unix goes much further. In Unix, the entire line-by-line program to run the OS is visible to programmers. Not only is it visible, but users can change it and customize it however they want. Customizers must, however, publish their customizations so other people can copy them.

Thanks to the open-source model, there are 31 different "flavors" of Unix.[5]

---

[4]Steven Johnson, *supra* note 2.

[5]Holman W. Jenkins Jr., "Not Enough Bleepin' Innovation?" *Wall Street Journal*, April 12, 2000, page A27.

Many of the large business computer vendors have their own particular flavors of Unix—such as Sun's Solaris Unix-based operating system. Unix is a lot of fun for people who like to write computer code and for people who want to customize an operating system for unique or complex tasks. On the other hand, Unix can be a nightmare for a small company that wants to write software applications. There is no guarantee that a program written for one flavor of Unix will run reliably—or will run at all—on other Unix flavors. By contrast, the software developer can write a program just once for standardized environments, such as Windows or the MacOS, and instantly have a program that will work properly on many millions of computers.

The Unix market is in some ways a utopian model of perfect competition. There are dozens of competitors (all of the different Unix flavors), and the program is free. The history of Unix, though, shows that not having a standard environment can impede software applications development. Unix is a great way to get an elegant operating system for a university's campuswide network, but until recently it was a terrible way to motivate programmers to write software applications.

Unix aficionados have overcome the non-standardization problem by adopting Linux (a Unix flavor written by Linus Torvalds) as the standard OS for desktop Unix applications. In 1998, when the Microsoft case began, 30 companies offered Linux pre-installed on computers. In May 2000, 78 did.[6] Many of the major hardware manufacturers—such as Dell, Compaq, Intel, and IBM—are supporting Linux in one way or another.[7]

Anyone who doubts that Linux is a viable, major operating systems competitor *today* need only walk down to the local computer store and see how much shelf space is devoted to Linux and Linux applications—in great contrast to May 1998, when the Microsoft antitrust case began. Large computer stores do not sell interesting products for computer geeks; they sell mass market products, and they keep those products in stock only because the products move off the shelves quickly. By mid-1999, retail sales of Linux were approximately equal to those of Windows 98 and, in some stores, Linux far outsells Windows 98.[8] Overall in 1999, Linux accounted for 17 percent of retail operating systems sales.[9]

---

[6]Wayne Crews, "Behind the Breakup Curve on Microsoft," *Washington Times*, May 22, 2000.

[7]*Ibid.*; Charles Babcock, "Linux Boosts Unix," *Inter@ctive Week*, October 23, 2000.

[8]Richard B. McKenzie, *Trust on Trial: How the Microsoft Case is Reframing the Rules of Competition* (Cambridge, MA: Perseus Books, 2000), page 52.

[9]Dori Jones Yang, "Laying in for the Long Siege," *U.S. News & World Report*, April 17, 2000, page 43.

The most important barrier to Linux proliferating on home or small office personal computers is the OS's difficulty. While Linux is robust once installed, installation is complex, and using Linux is not intuitively easy. Like DOS, Linux uses a command-line interface. That is why Linux is preferred among computer gurus who sneer at Windows, which emphasizes user-friendliness at the expense of code-writing elegance.

In May 2000, Mexican programmer Miguel de Icaza announced the creation of Gnome, a Linux shell that gives Linux the look and feel of Windows. Gnome is free, as is a Linux spreadsheet program, Gnumeric, which mimics Microsoft Excel for Windows. There is also an email program/personal organizer called Evolution, which Icaza calls "our Outlook-killer" and which can import data from the Microsoft Outlook email/personal organizer. As for the proposed breakup of Microsoft, says Icaza: "It stinks. I wanted to beat them without government assistance."[10]

Other companies are also working on an easy graphical interface for Linux. One such company, Silicon Valley's Eazel, points out that the personal computer made it nearly impossible for companies to bundle expensive hardware and software together. (The lone remaining exception is for certain high-end uses.) Now, the hardware and software are sold separately, and both are cheap. In the near future, open source may destroy the business models of both Microsoft and Apple, which are based on selling proprietary software.[11] Dell Computers has partnered with Eazel to install Eazel's software on Linux desktop machines.

Linux is a "disruptive" technology, argues IBM's vice president of Internet technology, John Patrick. As the PC disrupted the mainframe, Linux will disrupt today's operating systems, Patrick predicts.[12]

By late 1999, Linux had 15 million users.[13] The program is free, but customers pay to buy it from companies, such as Red Hat, in exchange for technical support and documentation. Thirty percent of Internet sites are run by Linux, as are 25 percent of office servers. So far, 4 percent of desktop computers are running Linux.[14]

---

[10]Thomas E. Weber, "Here's a Plan to End Microsoft's Dominance (No Lawyers Needed)," *Wall Street Journal*, May 15, 2000.

[11]"Open Sesame," *The Economist*, April 15, 2000, page 72.

[12]"IBM Sees Linux in Your Future," *Inter@ctive Week*, April 3, 2000, page 100.

[13]Steven Levy, "Judging Jackson by his Actions," *Newsweek*, November 22, 1999, page 68.

[14]"A Window of Opportunity for Linux," *U.S. News & World Report*, May 8, 2000, page 36.

"Ironically, beating Windows on the desktop is not the Holy Grail for most Linux executives. Instead, they want to dominate the faster-growing market for Web and Internet devices. 'Windows is a legacy system. It won't go away, but it's not the platform of choice,' says Ransom Love, CEO of Caldera Systems, a Linux service provider."[15]

THE DISAPPEARING PERSONAL COMPUTER

The history of computing is a history of unforeseen changes in the locus of power. IBM did not mind letting Bill Gates keep the property rights to the computer operating system known as DOS because IBM knew that, in the past, the key to computing control had been in the chip, which IBM still owned. Several influential techno-experts believe the locus of power now has begun another change:

> In an ironic twist, the judge declared Microsoft a monopoly at the very moment its dominance seems most threatened. Because of changing technology, the computer industry is now at what former Intel Chairman Andy Grove calls an "inflection point," a time when the balance of forces shifts to profound new ways of computing. Just as the introduction of the PC in the early 1980s signaled a shift from mainframes to desktop computers, now, pundits believe, the Internet and a proliferation of small computer devices promise to undermine the PC's supremacy. "I don't think that the PC is going away, but there are going to be a lot more appliances coming into the picture," says Gateway President Jeff Weitzen. "And there are going to be a lot more sold of them than PCs."[16]

Weitzen is probably correct, for not only will Internet appliances and the like proliferate, but ordinary appliances will start acting more like computers. As *U.S. News & World Report* summarizes:

> Someday, pundits predict, computers won't just sit on the desktop in your office. They will run on your television, stereo, refrigerator, washing machine, oven, cell phone, and car. Your microwave, for

---

[15] *Ibid.*

[16] Dori Jones Yang, "The Empire Strikes Out," *U.S. News & World Report*, November 15, 1999, page 48.

instance, may be able to check the Net to find out how long to cook that bag of peas. Rushing to the airport in your car, you might be able to ask your auto PC to rebook your flight. Today's market of 114 million PCs looks tiny compared with the billions of smaller computers that will someday run everything imaginable.[17]

In hindsight, Bill Gates made a major miscalculation in 1995 when he brought out a major new operating system (Windows 95) that paid scant attention to the Internet. Late in the year, Gates announced a major reorientation: Henceforth, Microsoft would be an Internet company.

Microsoft Windows for personal computers was made for an environment in which space was abundant (computers could be several feet tall), computing power was strong and getting stronger, and bandwidth (via narrow-band dial-up modems) was scarce. The future of computing appears to be evolving in precisely the opposite direction: Bandwidth is becoming plentiful and omnipresent (as in Internet connections via mobile phones). But available space (*e.g.*, the room for a circuit board in a cell phone) is scarce, and, consequently, computing power for the new devices is vastly less than what is needed for Windows 98 or Microsoft's latest OS, Windows ME.

Microsoft prospered by creating easy interfaces and giving the user lots of help—but at a heavy cost in computing power. The explosion of processing power and hard disk storage space at falling prices made Microsoft's strategy a winner during the 1990s. But the new computing environment may make Microsoft's accumulated expertise more of a hindrance than a help.

The organization and retrieval of information is already changing radically. From the pre-DOS era to the present, personal computers organized their information in structured directories, similar to groups of nesting file folders in a file cabinet. The information was accessed by using a keyboard or mouse to interact with a computer screen. In the new world of non-PC Internet devices, many of which are too small to accommodate a keyboard, the interface will be via voice recognition or some other means, and the accessed data will be scattered in many different places on the Internet, rather than on a single hierarchical disk drive.[18]

Scott McNealy, head of Sun Microsystems, predicts that by 2002 fewer than half of the devices that use the Internet will be PCs running Windows.[19]

---

[17]*Ibid.*, page 52.

[18] Todd Spangler, "Big Thinkers: Eric Freeman," *Inter@ctive Week*, April 24, 2000, page 50.

[19]David Ignatius, "Microsoft's Next Monopoly," *Washington Post*, June 13, 1999, page B7.

Likewise, Steve Case, head of AOL/Netscape, has announced his company will not bother competing against the Windows operating system, because "the PC operating system is increasingly irrelevant to the battles of the future."[20]

In short, the main reason companies like Sun and AOL/Netscape have not mounted a major frontal challenge to Microsoft's lead on the personal computer desktop is that the desktop represents the last war. The real battle is for the hundreds of millions of devices that will take computing far beyond the desktop.[21] Dominance of the desktop business may soon be no more important in the IT industry than dominance of the horseshoe business was in the transportation industry after 1925.

Some analysts divide the near-future world of computing into five main groups: personal computers—including desktops, palm-type devices, and Web-enabled telephones; television and other audio-visual devices such as game machines; kitchen and laundry appliances; home automation, such as temperature control and security; and the automobile. Let us briefly examine some of the best-known of the potential new computing devices.

Dumb Terminals
and Network Computers

If you went to college during the 1980s and wanted access to a computer, you could go to the university's computing center and wait for terminal time. When you cleared the waiting list, you would sit at a "dumb terminal"—a keyboard and monitor connected to the university mainframe, which did all the actual computing.

A few years ago, Sun and Oracle were predicting a return to this model in the form of the Network Computer (NC). A modern version of the old-fashioned dumb terminal, the NC would have no hard drive and would instead use applications from the Web written in Java. Such a computer would cost less than $1,000, and, the theory was, only Microsoft's unfair competition was blocking its development. But the NC never happened, primarily because the technological scenario on which the NC depended turned out to be almost exactly wrong.

The theory was that NCs would save their owners money because they would centralize storage and processing costs. But personal computer storage

---

[20]David Ignatius, "AOL Gets Ready to Rumble," *Washington Post*, July 25, 1999, page B7.

[21]Holman W. Jenkins Jr., "Netscape Hype: An Epilogue," *Wall Street Journal*, May 27, 1998.

costs (hard disk prices) fell precipitously, and processor power doubled every 18 months, thus obeying Moore's Law. The would-be NC, selling for less than $1,000, had to compete against a PC that was now available for less than $800. The PC could do everything the NC could do—and much, much more. And then, the price of a PC fell to zero for consumers willing to sign three-year contracts for $20 to $25 per month with an Internet Service Provider.

Computer hardware got better and cheaper too quickly for the NC to become viable. The one technological development the NC did require—plentiful bandwidth for NC-to-server connections—began to proliferate in businesses, but the very large majority of home computer users are still using 56k dial-up modem connections. When most of these home users choose to subscribe to broadband, perhaps in 2002 or later, the NC concept will be at least a decade old (in Internet Time).

Ironically, the companies backing the NC, such as Sun Microsystems, turn out to be pursuing a business plan similar to what they accused Microsoft of during the Microsoft antitrust trial. It is difficult to see how consumer choice and competition could flourish if consumers trade in their PCs and other computer devices for updated dumb terminals dependent on centralized business servers supplied by Sun and a few other companies.[22]

Still, the push for the NC continues, with Sun and Oracle announcing a licensing agreement they say will allow them to create computers that do not use an operating system.[23] Although dumb terminals/network computers/computers without an OS may one day be a major competitor to Windows, no such competition has developed yet.

Internet Appliances

The product that may fulfill the potential of the NC (without being as dumb as a dumb terminal) is the Internet appliance. This is a simplified computer, intended almost exclusively for email and the Web. The purchase price for these devices is low, but the buyer must agree to pay a monthly fee for Web access.

America Online and Gateway 2000, for example, have jointly introduced an Internet appliance small enough to sit on a kitchen counter for less than $500. Buyers purchase an ISP contract with America Online for approximately $22

---

[22]Richard B. McKenzie, *Trust on Trial, supra* note 8, page 188.

[23]"Sun Heats Up Oracle's Raw Iron," *Product News*, Oracle Corp., www.oracle.com/oramag/oracle/99-Mar/29prod.html. The network computers would be connected to a database server running Sun Solaris OS.

per month, which includes Web surfing, AOL's proprietary content, and email.[24] The Netpliance I-Opener sells for $99 plus $21.95/month in ISP charges.[25] For consumers who want an email device only, with no Web surfing, there are products such as the MailStation, which costs $99 plus $9.95 per month.[26]

The market for these products is not primarily the consumer who wants to buy a PC. After all, the price for an inexpensive PC with monitor is reasonably close to the $500 cost of the Gateway/AOL Internet appliance. Rather, the market is a consumer who *doesn't* want to buy a personal computer. Computer-resistant seniors and other folks who have convinced themselves they could never use a computer can get over their intimidation by buying a device, hardly larger than a radio, that sits on the kitchen counter and has an extremely simple interface.

The AOL/Gateway model runs on Linux with a graphical shell on top. Red Hat—the best-known Linux company—offers Linux software for Internet appliances. But Linux is not the only player in the appliance world. The new "Be" operating system (BeOS) is free for personal computers, but so far has achieved little market penetration among PC users. But Be is selling its OS for Internet appliance products being developed by Compaq and Intel. Wind River Systems is working to create a Java-based Internet appliance platform. Another operating system, QNX, sells to IBM, Motorola, and Netpliance. Microsoft is also attempting entry into the market with a "Web companion."

Smart Peripherals

As chip costs fall, peripheral devices are getting smarter. Ten Internet Years ago, a digital camera, scanner, or printer would need to be connected to a PC so that the PC's microchip could do the hard work of image manipulation. Today, one can print high-quality digital pictures with a digital camera and color printer without a PC. The camera and the printer each have enough internal computing power to do the work previously performed by the PC.

The evolution of the smart device continues the trend towards decentralizing computing power. Just as the mainframe or minicomputer did all the work for the dumb terminals to which it was attached, the PC did all the

---

[24]"You've Got Appliances," *Inter@ctive Week*, April 20, 2000, page 10.

[25]www.netpliance.com.

[26]www.mailstation.com.

work for printers, scanners, and other peripheral devices to which *it* was attached. Now, the dissemination of computing power enables those devices to compute for themselves. A printer or digital camera that can think for itself is computationally and practically independent of the PC and the PC's OS.

Telephones, PDAs, and Mobile Devices

So far, the largest number of new non-PC devices taking over from PCs are Portable (or "Personal") Digital Assistants (PDAs) such as 3Com's Palm Pilot. Microsoft makes a PDA called the Pocket PC that runs the Windows CE operating system. Windows CE duplicates the look and feel of the desktop Windows, allowing software writers who create CE programs to use many of the same techniques used for desktop Windows.

Does Microsoft's leverage of its desktop Windows power give it an unfair advantage in the market for handheld operating systems? Hardly. *Inter@ctive Week* explains: "Years from now, Microsoft's Windows 2000 launch might be likened to IBM's introducing a huge sparkling mainframe at the dawn of the PC industry: a big deal, but an albatross at the same time. . . . The latest iteration of Windows is titanic compared to the lightweight code that's required to run the flotilla of gadgets and appliances expected to flood the electronics market this year and next."[27] Or, as a Goldman, Sachs analyst warned as he downgraded the stock's rating, "There is an increasing risk that Microsoft might atrophy on the PC platform as IBM did on the mainframe platform, while robust growth shifts to handheld and wireless devices."[28]

For handheld devices shipped in 1998, the Palm OS accounted for 83.5 percent, and Windows CE for only 9.7 percent.[29] The Palm Pilot reached one million users faster than any other computing device in history.[30] As Microsoft did with desktop Windows, Palm has built a large cadre of independent developers who want to write for the Palm OS. The 30,000

---

[27]"Net Devices: Can Windows Shrink to Fit?" *Inter@ctive Week*, February 14, 2000, page 91.

[28]Dori Jones Yang, "Are Baby Bills in Our Future?" *U.S. News & World Report*, May 8, 2000, page 34.

[29]"Net Devices: Can Windows Shrink to Fit?" *supra* note 27, pages 91-92. In 2000, Microsoft introduced a third handheld device, after the failure of the first two. By the end of the year, Microsoft had 18 percent of the market, compared to Palm's 74 percent. "Pocket PC Devices Making Headway Against Palm," *Bloomberg News*, November 28, 2000.

[30]Rich Karlgaard, "Fat, Florid, Farcical," *Forbes*, November 29, 1999, page 51.

developers working on the Palm OS are a large barrier to entry by another mobile OS, Palm's founder suggests.[31] Palm is trying to be the "OS of choice" for all handheld devices, including phones, audio players, and game machines.[32]

Recent developments are making mobile devices much more than just compact Filofaxes. Collapsible, easily portable keyboards make word processing and other input-intensive functions on the PDAs much easier. The potential development of speech recognition, allowing small device users to bypass the keyboard altogether, will make the PDAs still more accessible.

Almost all of the PDAs have modems (sometimes built-in, sometimes attached) for surfing the Internet and using email. The Palm VII provides wireless Internet surfing. PDAs are converging with digital phones. For example, consumers using a Sprint PCS phone (or similar phones from other companies) can send and receive email, buy a book from Amazon.com, trade stocks, get point-to-point driving directions, or get news, weather, and sports from dozens of sources.

Foreseeing the proliferation of speech recognition on PDAs and digital phone Web browsers, over two dozen companies are working to develop "voice portals." A voice portal such as Yahoo!, for example, might be accessible from an 800 number dialed on a digital phone. Without ever touching a keyboard, the consumer would be able to use the voice portal to retrieve customized stock quotes, restaurant guides for whatever part of town he is calling from, and much more. Like Internet appliances, the voice portals may eventually help overcome barriers to computer use; not everyone thinks he can use a computer, but almost everyone knows how to use a phone by speaking into the mouthpiece.[33]

"Every so often, there are disruptive technologies. The PC was one, the Internet was one, and we look at wireless Internet as the next disruptive technology," suggests Jon Roberts of the venture capital firm, Ignition.[34] "For many people, the telephone is going to end up being the computer," predicts Irwin Jacobs, founder of Qualcomm.[35]

While the Department of Justice continues to litigate about what happened in the desktop "browser war" between Netscape and Microsoft, the "new browser war" on digital phones is being fought by companies such as Symbian

---

[31]Bonnie Guglielmo, "Handspring Could Roll Its Own OS," *Inter@ctive Week*, February 28, 2000, page 100.

[32]Todd Spangler, "Palm's Future Is in Its Own Hands," *Inter@ctive Week*, February 28, 2000, page 95.

[33]"Talking to the Internet," *Newsweek*, April 24, 2000, page 69.

[34]Peg McGinity, "Ignition to Spark Wireless Net," *Inter@ctive Week*, March 27, 2000, page 59.

[35]William J. Holstein, "The Ex-professor's High Wireless Act," *U.S. News & World Report*, May 8, 2000, page 38.

(the EPOC browser) and Phone.com (the UP browser). Neither Netscape nor Microsoft is a significant player.[36]

The Bluetooth protocol, developed by 500 companies jointly, specifies a common standard for the PDAs and digital phones. By 2001, most new PDAs and digital cell phones will carry the $5 Bluetooth chip, allowing them to exchange data wirelessly with larger devices (*e.g.*, laptop or desktop computers) or other small devices that have the chip.[37] Just as today's Internet uses the common but non-proprietary standards of HTML and TCP/IP, many small devices are adopting the Wireless Application Protocol (WAP) as a common standard for their own Internet connections.[38] By 2003, digital data cell phones may outnumber personal computers.[39]

Today's cell phones communicate with radio towers or satellites with one of two protocols: CDMA and TDMA. Efforts are underway to combine these protocols, which will then allow an American cell phone to be used in Europe. For both mobile devices and other appliances, the operating system is much less visible to the consumer than it is on a personal computer. Thus, explains industry analyst Joyce Becknell of the Aberdeen Group, Microsoft loses the advantage it had enjoyed on desktops, since Internet appliance users are no more interested in the operating system than television watchers are in the details of broadcasting.[40]

Home Appliances

The closest that near-future home computing comes to *The Jetsons* is the burgeoning interest in "smart appliances" with Internet connections. If a homeowner had a smart furnace thermostat, she could order the heat turned up before she left her office to drive home. A smart electrical system would accept orders for lights to be turned on, the oven to start warming up, and so forth.

Smart appliances are well-suited to customizable operating systems such as

---

[36]Alan Reynolds, "An Unsettling Antitrust Case," *National Review Online*, April 3, 2000, http://www.nationalreview.com/comment/comment 040300c.html.

[37]"Tomorrow's Internet," *The Economist*, November 13, 1999, page 24.

[38]*Ibid.*

[39]Marion Long, "Stuart Feldman Pushing the Internet Time Envelope," *Inter@ctive Week*, January 10, 2000, page 90.

[40] "Net Devices: Can Windows Shrink to Fit?" *supra* note 27.

Unix. In Japan, Matsushita, Sony, and other companies are working together to develop consistent standards, so appliances can communicate even if they use different operating systems.[41] This kind of collaboration might be considered an antitrust problem in the United States, but Japan has no antitrust laws. The Japanese collaboration reduces the possibility that Microsoft, Sun, or some other company will be able to impose an operating system on home appliances.

Television-Based Computing and Game Machines

Before computerized home appliances become widespread, many homes will have one or more game machines that do some of the work currently performed by personal computers. Such products are currently being introduced. The Sega Dreamcast has built-in networking and, like the Sony Playstation 2 (which has a DVD drive), includes a microprocessor, ports, and user controls—all the essentials of a small multipurpose computer. Indeed, the Playstation 2 can perform 6.2 billion floating operations per second, as many as a high-end PC.[42] A television substitutes for the monitor.

Of course, the *primary* use for these machines is playing games. For the machines to offer real-time action games with lots of graphics over the Internet—a potential revenue stream for companies that formerly made no more money once the game was sold—the user will usually need a faster connection than can be provided by a dial-up modem. Simpler, text-based games like Jeopardy will work with a dial-up modem.

Another form of computing comes from television set-top boxes that function as small computers for Web surfing and email. Microsoft has recognized the potential of television-based Web-surfing and computing, which is why the company bought WebTV several years ago. Sensibly, the Department of Justice did not block the acquisition, since the market barely existed. Several years later, Microsoft's WebTV has only a million subscribers.[43]

Today, Microsoft is creating a version of Windows customized for AT&T/TCI's cable boxes. IBM, TCI itself, and Sun are among the competitors

---

[41]Steven Butler, "Smart Toilets and Wired Refrigerators," *U.S. News & World Report*, June 7, 1999, page 48.

[42]Jeffrey Eisenach, Thomas Lenard, and Stephen McGonesá, *The Digital Economy Fact Book* (Washington, DC: Progress and Freedom Foundation, second edition, 2000), page 28.

[43]"Microsoft's WebTV Shuts Out Some Subscribers," *Bloomberg News*, September 27, 2000 (available at http://news.cnet.com/).

in this market.[44] AOL/Netscape is entering the television computing business, as part of its "AOL Anywhere" initiative. Compared to Microsoft, AOL/Netscape has been an order of magnitude more successful as a Web site operator and Internet Service Provider, so it would be foolish to underestimate AOL-TV's potential for turning a small market into a giant one.

While WebTV and similar devices turn televisions into Internet appliances, new products from AOL, Sony, and Sega could go much further. It would not be difficult for them to take on word processing and many other home computer tasks. Moreover, their pricing is well below even inexpensive PCs, even though their graphics are typically much better.[45] Television-based computers—both game machines and the others—could also serve as the foundation for computing in the rest of the home—providing the hub for smart appliances, Internet appliances, and other computing devices.

Microsoft's main hope in this arena is its "X-Box," which the company plans to introduce in late 2001. The X-Box can match the AOL, Sony, and Sega products as a multipurpose computing platform.

The X-box is not Microsoft's first foray into hardware, although the company (unlike Apple, Sun, and IBM) has never before tried to provide an all-in-one software solution to customers. In order to encourage sales of early versions of Windows, Microsoft made the first PC mouse, since PC users tended to think of mice (and hence, a graphical interface) as an Apple-only product. Microsoft still makes mice and keyboards, and gives them special features designed to take advantage of Windows; Microsoft's market share for these input devices is respectable but not dominant, as a tour of the aisles of computer stores will attest.

Under the Department of Justice's breakup plan for Microsoft, an operating system company would be separated from the rest of the company and would be forbidden to integrate the OS into new products without prior approval from the government. Those constraints would seem to rule out the X-Box project. Sega, Sony, and AOL/Netscape would benefit substantially from restrictions on a competitor in an important emerging market.

Judge Jackson rejected all evidence about alternative computing devices, because no device does everything a PC does. The judge's theory ignores the fact that many consumers do not need or want everything a PC does.

Computing is already moving far beyond the boundaries of the desktop PC,

---

[44]Dawn Kawamato, "Are Investors Ready to Tune in on Interactive TV?" http://news.cnet.com/, September 25, 2000.

[45]The interlacing standards for the lines on television screens are much better for graphics, but not as good as computer monitors for fine tasks such as intensive word processing or spreadsheet work.

as Internet-only devices and devices that replace personal computers begin to take off. To worry in the year 2000 that Microsoft will own the future of computing because of its strong position in the desktop PC market is like worrying in 1938 that the Mutual Broadcasting System would own the future of electronic entertainment because of its strong position in radio.

SOFTWARE MOVES OFF THE DISK

Web-based Applications

Just as the personal computer faces competition from a new breed of computing devices, it also must compete with a former ally: the Internet. Many functions once reserved exclusively for the PC are migrating to the Web.

Several Web-based companies, for example, now offer data backup on the Web. Rather than purchase a Zip drive, tape drive, or other backup hardware, a PC user can store critical backup files on the Internet with companies such as Driveway, Yahoo!, FreeSpace, I-Drive, and Connected Online Backup.[46] Typically, these companies offer around 30 megabytes of backup for free, with more available for purchase. Besides reducing the need for hardware backup peripherals, these online storage services also make it easier for Web users to share music and other files with friends or colleagues.

Software applications are also migrating to the Internet.[47] Many Web portals such as Yahoo!, Excite, and AOL/Netscape, as well as specialized sites like AnyDay, offer services such as calendars, address books, email, and maps with point-to-point driving directions, all of which formerly existed mainly on hard disks. Even encyclopedias and other reference applications are now on the Web.

What all of these Web applications have in common is that they rely on the common Web standard of HTML. With HTML as the *lingua franca*, it does not matter whether the personal computer is running Windows, Linux, or MacOS, or whether the PC uses an Intel-compatible chip or a Motorola chip.

As anyone who uses Web-based email over a dial-up modem connection knows, Web-based services are not, today, always delivered to the computer as rapidly as would be ideal. The spread of always-on broadband connections will make Web-based services more popular, as will the development of more complex Web-based programs, such as sophisticated word processing.

---

[46] www.connected.com.

[47] For a list of current business applications, see www.apps.com.

Software on the Chip

Besides moving out to the Internet, software is also moving down to the chip. Intel, the leading microprocessor manufacturer for Windows-based PCs, is building enhancement for voice recognition onto its chips rather than letting software handle voice processing. According to one Internet consultant, Mark Tebbe of Lante Corp., "Microsoft and Intel were an unstoppable force when they were arm-in-arm. The fact that each is going its own separate way is one of the biggest shifts that Microsoft has ever had to face."[48]

Microsoft may attempt to discourage Intel's plan (as a rational company should), since future editions of Windows would have to run one way to interact with Intel chips that provide voice recognition, and another way to interact with chips from other companies that do not.

HOW MICROSOFT IS RESPONDING

Microsoft's response to the changes in technologies and rise of new competitors is the strongest possible evidence that the Windows PC era is coming to an end. Microsoft's newest OS, dubbed Microsoft.NET, will allow information-sharing across the Web and across different devices.[49] Simply put, Microsoft had to dramatically change its operating system model in order to keep up with computer changes. "Essentially, the development of Internet applications, and the growth of the applications service provider industry, have pulled Microsoft's traditional operating system platform out from under it," explained *The Industry Standard*.[50]

Today, a consumer who wants to access her financial information goes to one Web site for her bank, another for her broker, a third for her credit card, and so on. She can access these Web sites fairly readily from a personal computer, but access from a PDA or digital phone is often awkward, if even possible at all. With Microsoft.NET, software would consolidate all of the individual's financial information from various sources and would present that information in a simple report that could be read from a PC, PDA, digital phone, or any

---

[48]"The Tech Boom Will Keep Rocking," *Fortune*, February 15, 1999, page 78.

[49]"Winternet," *The Economist*, July 1, 2000, pages 62-63. The "dot net" project is also called "Next Generation Windows Services" (NGWS).

[50]Dominic Gates, "How to Integrate Everything," *The Industry Standard*, May 22, 2000, page 121.

other device.[51]

What makes Microsoft.NET radically different from past Microsoft OSs is that the company does not plan to write the program in C++ language, the programming language proprietary to Microsoft that cannot be read by outsiders. Instead, Microsoft.NET will be, like Unix, open source code, and it will be written in Extensible Markup Language (XML), the successor to Hypertext Markup Language (HTML).

Nobody owns HTML, but the 400-member World Wide Web Consortium develops new standards for it. Standards for XML are set by the same consortium, which includes Microsoft and its rivals Oracle, IBM, and Sun.

Once the universal standards are set, companies may add supplements, which they hope will eventually be broadly adopted. Microsoft and Netscape (the latter more than the former) both attempted their own additions to HTML, although neither company seemed able to make much difference in the language's evolution.

While adhering to the XML standards, Microsoft plans to add its own elaborations to Microsoft.NET in XML, and those elaborations will work best with computers running Windows. There's no guarantee, of course, that consumers will find Microsoft's version of XML compelling; there will be plenty of other versions, each with its own elaborations, from companies such as Hewlett-Packard (the "e-speak" project) and many of the other 400 members of the WWW Consortium. Forrester Research predicts Microsoft will not be able to adapt to an open-source world, and will eventually shrink to a "legacy vendor" for older software.[52]

BRIEFLY STATED . . .

Microsoft faces serious competition from companies offering software and hardware products that weren't even invented 10 Internet Years ago, when the Department of Justice filed its suit against the company. Competitors include names familiar to those who followed the antitrust trial—AOL, Netscape, Sun, and Oracle—but many new names have been added to the list: Sega, Sony, Red Hat, Symbian, Phone.com, Netpliance, AT&T/TCI, 3Com, Yahoo!, Excite, and even Microsoft's former ally, Intel.

Some, like Red Hat, are using Linux to compete with Microsoft head-to-

---

[51]Brent Schlender, "Full Speed Ahead," *Fortune*, July 10, 2000, page 97.

[52]Michelle Delio, "It'll Be an Open-Source World," *Wired News*, August 15, 2000.

head for control of the PC operating system market. Others work to shrink that market by using non-PC devices to do what PCs used to do, and by writing programs in languages that can be read by computers using any operating system, not only Windows.

It was perhaps plausible 10 years ago (Internet Time) to allege that Microsoft was a monopoly, an issue addressed in greater detail below. But it is indisputable today that Microsoft faces intense competition from more directions than ever before. The rationale for treating Microsoft as a monopolist is evaporating with each passing month as the old battleground of the desktop PC becomes less and less relevant to consumers and to the IT industry.

An apt analogy to what is taking place in the world of computing may be found in the world of geopolitics. Cape Horn, on the southern-most tip of South America, was a location of enormous strategic importance before the opening of the Panama Canal. Once the Panama Canal opened, control over Cape Horn became a matter of little consequence. Similarly, whatever market power Microsoft may have had by virtue of its dominance in the PC operating system marketplace in May 1998 was vastly diminished by late 2000.

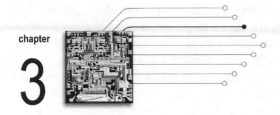

3

The Microsoft Monopoly

MONOPOLY AND THE SHERMAN ACT

When Adam Smith wrote *The Wealth of Nations*, everyone knew what a monopoly was: a privilege granted by the government to protect a business from competition; in exchange, the business shared its profits with the government.[1] For example, in 1631, the King of England granted certain people the exclusive privilege to make soap from vegetable oil. In exchange for that privilege, the soap-makers would give the King a certain amount of money for every ton of soap made.[2]

It was commonly understood that without the coercive force of government, no monopoly could exist. So in 1624, Parliament passed the Statute of Monopolies, which sharply limited the King's power to grant monopolies in

---

[1]Adam Smith, *An Inquiry into the Nature and Causes of the Wealth of Nations* (Indianapolis, IN: Liberty Classics, 1981 [1776]), Book 1, Chapter 10, Part 2; Book 4, Chapters 2 and 4.

[2]Cicely Veronica Wedgwood, *The Great Rebellion: The King's Peace, 1637-1641* (London, England: Collins, 1955). For more on popular and Parliamentary resistance to royal monopolies, see Michael Conant, "Antimonopoly Tradition Under the Ninth and Fourteenth Amendments: *Slaughterhouse Cases* Re-examined," 31 *Emory Law Journal* 785 (1982).

domestic commerce or manufacture. Likewise, many American state constitutions of the Early Republic contained explicit bans on "monopolies." Those provisions were aimed at controlling the abuse of government power.[3]

Today, government-created monopolies are still with us. Since the 1840s, it has been against the law for anyone to compete with the U.S. Postal Service by carrying first-class mail. Similarly, a person who has an exclusive patent granted by the Patent Office has a monopoly on the product produced with the patent for a certain period of time. Likewise, software creators, Microsoft included, may copyright their creations under a federal statute that grants a legally authorized monopoly on the use of intellectual property.

Since 1890, when Congress, following the lead of a few states, enacted a statute aimed at outlawing monopolies between or among companies (other than government-created monopolies)[4], definitions have changed in a confusing and often unpredictable way.[5]

Section One of the Sherman Act

Section One of the Sherman Antitrust Act outlaws *every* contract, conspiracy, or combination in "restraint of trade." The statute does not say that some companies may restrain trade, while others may not. Rather, the statute says *no one* may contract, conspire, or combine to restrain trade. Whatever a restraint of trade is, it is universally forbidden by the Sherman Act.[6]

Read according to its language, Section One of the Sherman Act makes almost every business guilty of a "restraint of trade." For example, a manufacturer might sell products only to authorized distributors whose personnel take classes familiarizing themselves with the company's products. A movie distributor might rent R-rated movies only to theaters that promise to demand identification from teenagers in order to ensure they were the appropriate age for admittance. Each of these acts is obviously a "restraint of trade." The manufacturer and movie distributor are restraining themselves from

---

[3]Lord Thomas Macaulay's classic *History of England* traced much of the public's resistance to unlimited search and seizure to the public's attempt to evade government monopoly trade restrictions.

[4]Also exempted from the Sherman Act are so-called "lawful monopolies" such as trade associations.

[5]15 U.S. Code §§ 1-7 (as amended).

[6]"Every contract, combination in the form of trust or otherwise, or conspiracy, in restraint of trade or commerce among the several States, or with foreign nations, is declared to be illegal."

dealing with some customers, and the movie distributor is restraining 13-year-old would-be consumers of R-rated movies.

Section One of the Sherman Act, therefore, is like a statute that says, "It shall be a felony for anyone to act unkindly." Since almost everyone violates the statute at some time, prosecutors have wide discretion to bring a case against almost anyone. Since everyone is guilty, prosecutors have ample discretion to decide whom they will prosecute and what types of unkindness (or restraint of trade) they will proceed against.

Section Two of the Sherman Act

Section Two of the Sherman Act is different. It states:

> Every person who shall monopolize, or attempt to monopolize, or combine or conspire with any other person or persons, to monopolize any part of the trade or commerce among the several States, or with foreign nations, shall be deemed guilty of a felony, and, on conviction thereof, shall be punished by fine not exceeding $10,000,000 if a corporation, or, if any other person, $350,000, or by imprisonment not exceeding three years, or by both said punishments, in the discretion of the court.

Adam Smith would have thought this Section could be violated by someone who petitioned Congress, "Please make it illegal for anyone except me to conduct a particular kind of commerce." He might have pointed to lobbying by postal workers, which helps preserve laws protecting the postal workers' monopoly in the delivery of first-class mail.

Of course, the Sherman Act has nothing to do with restraining classical monopolies. Instead, the Sherman Act is interpreted to mean that things ordinary businesses do—such as cut prices, raise prices, attempt to gain market share, and enter into mutually beneficial agreements with other companies—are illegal if performed by a monopoly.[7] Since the Sherman Act provides no guidance about what kind of business practices constitute "monopolize, or attempt to monopolize," the nature of prohibited conduct changes from year to

---

[7]Section Two "permits challenges to conduct that would be normal business practices if carried out by a firm that did not have monopoly power." Chris E. Hall and Robert E. Hall, *National Policy on Microsoft: A Neutral Perspective* (version 2.0, 1999), page 50, www.NetEcon.com.

year, depending on the theories of the Antitrust Division of the Department of Justice and the Federal Trade Commission. Precisely what is prohibited is not announced in advance, but instead must be discerned by monitoring DOJ and FTC enforcement proceedings. Because the Sherman Act is so broad and so vague, it provides a perfect opportunity for government officials to select targets based on political considerations.

As Federal Reserve Chairman Alan Greenspan explains, antitrust is:

> [A] world in which competition is lauded as the basic axiom and guiding principle, yet "too much" competition is condemned as "cutthroat." . . . It is a world in which the law is so vague that businessmen have no way of knowing whether specific actions will be declared illegal until they hear the judge's verdict—after the fact.[8]

How is a company to know when it is a "monopoly" and therefore required to cease many ordinary business practices? In truth, it is impossible, given the elastic, debatable definitions of what the "relevant market" is for any given product.

Significantly, the legal determination that a company possesses monopoly power is made only by a judge, based on evidence in the record. In the case of Microsoft, such a finding was made in November 1999. Because of that decision, acts performed by Microsoft from as long ago as 1994 became retroactively illegal, and the judge ordered Microsoft punished for its newly illegal acts.

This retroactive punishment is clearly the product of an "*ex post facto* Law."[9] Supposedly, in 1994, the employees of Microsoft should have known their company was a monopoly, thereby forecasting the judge's decision five years hence. The imputed foresight should have made those employees cease their ordinary business practices from 1994 onward. As one ex-employee complained, "Nobody ever told us that the monopoly switch had been turned on, that we were supposed to change the way we did things."[10]

There is another, even stranger aspect to the Sherman Act's new monopoly concept, exemplified in Judge Thomas Penfield Jackson's Microsoft ruling: The Sherman Act allows the government to revert to the kind of conduct Parliament tried to outlaw in 1624 and which so many American state constitutions forbid.

---

[8]Quoted in Thomas J. DiLorenzo, "Antitrust," in *Cato Handbook for Congress: 105th* (Washington, DC: Cato Institute, 1997), page 400.

[9]The Supreme Court has held that the Constitution's prohibition on "*ex post facto* Laws" applies only to cases involving criminal penalties, not civil ones. *Calder v. Bull,* 3 U.S. 386 (1798).

[10]Joseph Nocera, "I Remember Microsoft," *Fortune,* July 10, 2000, page 128.

The Sherman Act allows the federal government to act on behalf of various politically favored businesses by intervening in the free market to suppress competition against those politically favored businesses. And ironically, this suppression of competition is carried out in the name of *fighting* monopoly.

"Monopoly means consumers have no choices, not that too many consumers prefer the same product."[11] For every product for which Microsoft is alleged to possess monopoly power, consumers have other choices. Microsoft's market shares reflect consumer preference, not the absence of consumer choice.

WINDOWS OPERATING SYSTEMS

In the early days of personal computing, 90 percent of computers used the CP/M operating system. The so-called "applications barrier to entry" (more on this below) should have prevented any new operating system from displacing CP/M, since there were far more applications for CP/M than any other operating system. But IBM and Microsoft jointly developed DOS (Disk Operating System), which was superior and quickly displaced CP/M.[12] One of the ways IBM and Microsoft overcame the CP/M "applications barrier to entry" was by underpricing; CP/M cost $240, while DOS was sold for $40.[13]

When DOS was introduced, most operating systems were sold bundled with hardware. The only way to buy the operating system was to buy the hardware that went with it. Apple is the most notable surviving practitioner of this software-hardware integration strategy for PCs. The innovative practice of separating OS control from the hardware attracted plenty of "clone" manufacturers of IBM-compatible computers who wanted to give customers an inexpensive operating system pre-installed with the hardware. The proliferation of these clones, in turn, encouraged more and more software developers to write programs for DOS.[14]

In the mid-1980s, Microsoft introduced Windows, a graphical interface to

---

[11]Alan Reynolds, "What Monopoly?" *National Review Online*, June 7, 2000.

[12]David S. Evans and Richard L. Schmalensee, "Be Nice to Your Rivals: How the Government is Selling an Antitrust Case without Consumer Harm in *United States v. Microsoft*," in David S. Evans, Franklin M. Fisher, Daniel L. Rubinfeld, and Richard L. Schmalensee, *Did Microsoft Harm Consumers? Two Opposing Views* (Washington, DC: AEI-Brookings Joint Center for Regulatory Studies, 2000), page 68.

[13]Richard B. McKenzie, *Trust on Trial: How the Microsoft Case is Reframing the Rules of Competition* (Cambridge, MA: Perseus, 2000), page 79.

[14]Microsoft had won a great deal of developer loyalty in the 1970s with a popular version of the BASIC programming language, written by Gates. Brent Schlender, "Full Speed Ahead," *Fortune*, July 10, 2000, page 106.

run on top of DOS. Windows 1.0 and 2.0 were failures and attracted few consumers or applications. Yet Bill Gates "bet the company" with Windows 3.0. When independent software developers were initially reluctant to write Windows applications, Gates had Microsoft software writers create Excel for Windows, which the computer industry press quickly acknowledged as the best spreadsheet on the market.

Windows 3.0 (1989) and 3.1 (1991) faced intense competition from IBM, which expected that its OS/2 would be the dominant graphical operating system. At the time, IBM was far larger than Microsoft. But IBM priced OS/2 very high ($240) and included no support for CD-ROM drives or small office networks, which were supported by Windows 3.11. Moreover, IBM charged independent software developers $600 for an OS/2 software development kit, while Microsoft distributed Windows kits for free. Many more developers chose to write for Windows than for OS/2. Thus, Windows 3.1 began to pull far ahead of OS/2 as the operating system chosen by most consumers—even though IBM, as a PC manufacturer, could bundle OS/2 with its hardware, while Microsoft had no Microsoft PCs with which Windows could be bundled. Windows 95 was superior to OS/2 in almost every respect. For all practical purposes, OS/2 disappeared after the successful introduction of Windows 95.

This was how Windows achieved its leading position in the operating systems market—by selling better products cheaper. The high-volume/low-price model Microsoft used for DOS has been the company's model ever since. The Justice Department and Judge Jackson both acknowledged that Microsoft's operating systems "monopoly" was built through superior business acumen and innovation and not in violation of any law.

But does Microsoft really have a monopoly in the operating systems market? Judge Jackson said yes, based on his finding that "Microsoft's share of the market for Intel-compatible PC operating systems "has been at least ninety-five percent."[15]

The 95 percent figure comes from a 1997 *forecast* of what the computer market would look like—a prediction made by International Data Corporation (IDC).[16] In fact, IDC's forecast was quite wrong, because IDC did not foresee the rise of Linux. For retail sales to consumers in February 2000, Windows operating systems of all types (95/98/NT) accounted for 77 percent of sales,

---

[15]Findings of Fact, *United States v. Microsoft*, no. 98-1232 (TPJ) (D.D.C. November 5, 1999) [hereinafter, "Jackson Findings of Fact"], ¶ 35.

[16]Alan Reynolds, "The Monopoly Myth," *Wall Street Journal*, April 9, 1999.

Linux for 17 percent, and the MacOS for 5 percent.[17]

Even to reach the 95 percent figure based on the flawed 1997 forecast, Judge Jackson and the DOJ had to include only operating systems for Intel-compatible chips—thus excluding personal computers that use other chips. The most prominent of these are Apple Computers, which use Motorola chips. Because Apple is excluded by Judge Jackson and DOJ as a competitor of Microsoft, Apple's iMac could capture 75 percent of new computer sales without affecting Microsoft's 95 percent "monopoly" figure. Because Apple is suggesting that its next operating system, OsX, will run on Intel chips, even the Department of Justice may have to admit that Apple competes with Microsoft.

All homes that run Windows, and most small offices that do so, run Windows 98 (or its successor, Windows ME; or one of its predecessors, Windows 95/3.1/3.0). Microsoft also makes another Windows operating system, Windows NT, meant solely for businesses running their computers on a network (and usually a network larger than the little networks Windows 98 can handle). In the world of business-networked computers, Windows NT has approximately a 32 percent market share, with most of the rest of the market going to some version of Unix.[18]

The 95 percent figure is achieved by *including* all computers that run on Windows NT, but *excluding* all computers that run on competitors to NT.[19] Among those excluded are desktop computers from Sun Microsystems, which run on SPARC-compatible chips, as well as Unix-based computers that run on Intel chips.[20] By mid-2000, International Data Corporation pegged Microsoft's share of operating system sales at 66 percent—a far cry from the 95 percent prediction (made in 1997) that Judge Jackson treated as fact.[21]

The 95 percent figure also ignores the fact that 15 percent of new personal computers are sold "naked"—without an operating system.[22] Some buyers of naked systems simply buy an operating system disk (*e.g.*, Microsoft Windows or Red Hat Linux) and install it themselves. But many other buyers get a naked system so they can avoid paying for the operating system entirely. They can

---

[17]Rob Kaiser, "Computer Users to Notice Ruling," *Chicago Tribune*, April 4, 2000, page 1.

[18]Alan Reynolds, "The Monopoly Myth," *supra* note 16.

[19]*Ibid.*

[20]*Ibid.*

[21]Richard McKenzie, "Microsoft's 'Applications Barrier to Entry': The Missing 70,000 Programs," *Policy Analysis* No. 380 (Washington, DC: Cato Institute, 2000), page 17, note 5.

[22]Alan Reynolds, "The Monopoly Myth," *supra* note 16.

either install a free version of Linux or BeOS, or, more commonly, a pirated copy of Windows (*e.g.*, a copy borrowed from a friend).

Microsoft's fear of provoking software piracy is one of the things that keeps Windows prices low. If Microsoft charges computer manufacturers (original equipment manufacturers, or OEMs) $50 a copy for Windows and the cost is passed on to consumers, most consumers will be too honest, or too uninterested in software installation, to bother buying a naked machine and obtaining pirated software. But if Microsoft raised the price of Windows to a true monopoly price of $900 (more on this below) or even $250, piracy would abound. Software piracy is illegitimate but real, and it is an important real constraint on Microsoft's ability to raise prices.

Another competitor to Microsoft's present sales is Microsoft's past sales. Whenever Microsoft offers an operating system upgrade, the company must convince consumers and business users to upgrade their installed base. It appears the majority of users choose *not* to upgrade. For example, as of 1999, only 16 percent of people using Intel-compatible personal computers had upgraded to Windows 98. Over 40 percent were still using Windows 95, and 20 percent were still using Windows 3.1/3.0, or DOS.[23] The rest were using a non-Microsoft operating system.

Also excluded from the 95 percent factoid are products such as game machines and Internet appliances, described in Chapter 2, which provide all or some of the functions of PCs and which do not run on the Windows 98 OS.

Appellate courts will reverse a trial court's finding of fact only if that finding is "clearly erroneous." Trial Judge Jackson's 95 percent "finding"—based on some very questionable massaging of numbers derived from an inaccurate forecast made in 1997—is clearly erroneous. Should the phony 95 percent figure fall, then along with it falls the legal conclusion that Microsoft Windows is a "monopoly." And when that conclusion falls, so do almost all of the antitrust violations of which Microsoft was convicted, for Section Two of the Sherman Act outlaws various forms of business conduct *only* when the business is a monopoly.

The Applications
Barrier to Entry

For a monopoly to exist, there must a strong "barrier to entry." For example, if the government threatens to imprison anyone who competes with the King's

---

[23]International Data Corporation survey discussed in Richard B. McKenzie, *Trust on Trial*, *supra* note 13, page 62.

preferred soap manufacturers, there is a strong barrier to entry. Similarly, if the only way in or out of an isolated town in a steep mountain valley is through a narrow path, and if the path is owned by a railroad that has installed train tracks on it, there would be a strong barrier to entry for competing railroads.

At first glance, it would seem the software business would not have strong barriers to entry. Would-be competitors need only write the software and sell it in computer stores, via Internet downloads, or by mail-order. The capital requirements for software production are relatively low, and the product itself is compact and easily transported on compact disks or over the Internet. Under antitrust theory, market share alone is not a barrier to entry, and therefore not proof that Microsoft is a monopoly.

The government's position on this matter, which Judge Jackson adopted, is that there is an "applications barrier to entry." Because there are so many applications written for Windows, the theory goes, other operating systems cannot compete, because there are fewer applications written for them.[24] This is a sophisticated way of saying Microsoft has done a better job than other companies encouraging developers to write for its OSs, and that this success should be regarded as malign. This is a fine example of how, in antitrust theory, the better a company competes the more likely its actions are to be called anti-competitive.

If Windows is a monopoly, and application developers have no choice but to write for it, why does Microsoft spend $650 million annually, using 2,000 employees, to provide support for independent software developers?[25] Microsoft appears to worry that if developers *don't* receive high-quality support for developing Windows applications, they may develop applications for another operating system. This hardly seems to be the behavior of a monopolist.

Putting aside the patent unfairness of the "applications barrier to entry" theory, the theory is patently false, as proven by the history of Windows itself.

By the early 1980s, DOS had emerged as the leading operating system for computers running the Intel chip. In 1993, DOS was sold with a larger fraction of Intel-compatible desktop computers than Windows is today.[26] Microsoft had written Windows 1.0 and Windows 2.0, graphical interfaces that ran on top of DOS. While DOS could run only one program at a time, Windows could run

---

[24]Jackson Findings of Fact, ¶ 40.

[25]David S. Evans and Richard L. Schmalensee, "The Economics of the Microsoft Antitrust Case: A Post-Trial Primer," in David S. Evans, Franklin M. Fisher, Daniel L. Rubinfeld, and Richard L. Schmalensee, *Did Microsoft Harm Consumers? Two Opposing Views, supra* note 12, page 71.

[26]That year, 79 percent of new Intel-compatible computers had Microsoft DOS, 13 percent had PC-DOS (from IBM), and 1 percent had DR-DOS (Digital Research), leaving only 4 percent for OS/2 and 1 percent for Unix. Kenneth C. Baseman, Frederick R. Warren-Boulton, and Glenn A. Woroch, "Microsoft Plays Hardball," *Antitrust Bulletin* 40: 265-315 (1995).

two or more Windows programs simultaneously.

Windows 1.0 and 2.0 were failures. Although Windows did attract some applications writers (there was a Windows version of the PageMaker desktop publishing program, and some developers of graphic-based games tried to use Windows), the number of Windows applications was tiny compared to those written for DOS.[27]

In 1989, Microsoft introduced Windows 3.0, promising that this time, Windows really would be powerful and useful. And it was. But what about the lack of applications? Microsoft introduced a new spreadsheet program, Excel, deemed best in its class by computer magazine reviewers. Microsoft also produced a Windows version of its word processing program, Word. The latter was not clearly superior to its competition, but it was as good as other leading products.

With Excel, a business or home user whose main work was on spreadsheets had a good reason to try Windows. Thanks to Word, he might be able to continue working in the Windows environment when he needed to write a business letter. Indeed, with Excel and Word, he could paste a chart from Excel into a business letter produced with Word.

Windows 3.1, introduced in 1991, made Windows more stable and added the ability to deal with new kinds of graphics programs as well as increasingly common new devices, such as CD-ROM drives. By 1994, many more applications were being written for Windows than for DOS.[28] If Windows could overcome DOS's gigantic lead in number of users and programmers, why does Windows' smaller lead in those areas now pose an impossible barrier to entry for OS/2, Linux, or MacOS?

Moreover, the applications barrier to entry is relevant only if the new OS is incompatible with software from the old OS. Consider the somewhat similar situation that prevailed when compact disk (CD) technology was introduced. The fact that everyone had record players and substantial investments in vinyl records did not stop them from adopting CDs. One reason is that buying a CD player did not mean the consumer had to give up his records all at once. The typical receiver had enough input jacks to accommodate both a turntable and a CD player. For any given listening session, the consumer could choose between vinyl and compact disk.

All versions of Windows have always been able to run DOS programs. Thus, consumers thinking about buying Windows 3.0 in 1990 knew they could

---

[27]Stan J. Liebowitz and Stephen E. Margolis, *Winners, Losers & Microsoft* (Oakland, CA: Independent Institute, 1999), pages 144-145.

[28]*Ibid.*, pages 145-146.

continue to use their existing DOS programs—and any new DOS programs that might be written—while *also* taking advantage of Windows and the smaller number of Windows applications.

In the late 1980s through the mid-1990s, IBM's OS/2 operating system competed in the consumer market with Windows. OS/2 could run OS/2 programs *and* Windows programs. Indeed, IBM boasted that OS/2 was "a better Windows than Windows."[29] So even though there were more Windows programs than OS/2 programs, IBM surmounted the "applications barrier to entry." OS/2 eventually lost to Windows due to IBM's mistake of pricing OS/2 much higher than Windows, failing to match Microsoft's aggressive support for independent application developers, and waiting too long to give OS/2 the ability to run CD-ROMs or participate in a small office network.

Today, the MacOS and Linux need only one supplemental program in order to be able to run any Windows application. Even without the supplemental program, Linux has the built-in capability to be installed in "dual-boot" mode. That is, when a PC owner turns on the computer, he can choose whether the computer will run Windows or Linux. The new BeOS can be installed to run in a Windows environment, allowing the user to run Windows programs and BeOS programs. Thus, the PC user can keep using current and future Windows applications, while also benefitting from whatever advantages Linux or BeOS or MacOS have to offer.

In short, the "applications barrier to entry" was never a barrier to the spread of new operating systems when consumers believed the new operating systems supplied something the dominant OS could not.

Finally, the government's assertion that Microsoft has a monopoly *because* of the applications "barrier" is self-contradictory.

On the one hand, the government claims Windows is a monopoly because there are supposedly so many applications (70,000)[30] written for Windows. Even Apple's MacOS is no threat to the monopoly, since it has only 12,000 applications, and neither is Linux, with just 2,500 applications.[31]

If the applications barrier to entry is insurmountable for Apple (12,000

---

[29]Joe Salemi, "OS/2 2.0: Does it Fulfill the Promise?" *PC Magazine*, April 28, 1992, page 165.

[30]The widely cited figure of 70,000 Windows applications is plainly erroneous. It includes every version of every program ever written for any version of DOS or Windows. When one counts only currently available programs, one finds there are about 2,000 current productivity applications for Windows, plus a few thousand game and entertainment programs. Of course, few computer users use more than a dozen programs. In short, another key "fact" upon which Judge Jackson found Microsoft to be a monopoly is plainly false. Ironically, one source of the inflated figures about the number of Windows applications was Microsoft's public relations department. See Richard McKenzie, "Microsoft's 'Applications Barrier to Entry': The Missing 70,000 Programs," *supra* note 21.

[31]www.linuxapps.com.

applications), *then* it must be equally insurmountable for Netscape and Java, which started with far fewer than 12,000 applications. Therefore, Netscape and Java are not relevant competitors to Windows, any more than Apple and Linux are. If they are not competitors, how could Microsoft's conduct toward them be labeled anti-competitive?

On the other hand, *if* Netscape and Java could overcome the Windows barrier to entry, *then* they are products that do compete with Windows. Accordingly, the market share calculation of Windows' relevant market should include data for sales of Netscape and Java, which would show that Windows' market share is far less than the 95 percent figure accepted by Judge Jackson, and Microsoft is not a monopoly.

When Microsoft takes action involving Java and Netscape, then Java and Netscape are competitors being harmed by Microsoft. But when determining that Microsoft is a monopoly (and therefore forbidden from taking anti-Netscape or anti-Java actions that an ordinary business would be allowed to do), then Netscape and Java do not count as competitors. It is impossible for all of the government's theory to be true at once.

Faced with the above argument, the government developed a fall-back position. (Since antitrust is so content-less, one can fall back to any position that is comfortable.) It was not actually Netscape and Java that would challenge the Windows monopoly. Rather, they would do the preliminary work of weakening the applications barrier to entry—by causing fewer developers to write Windows-only applications, as opposed to cross-platform Java/Netscape applications.

Then, somebody else (unknown) would come along and create a new operating system that would directly challenge the Windows monopoly. (Apparently the insurmountable applications barrier to entry of 70,000 Windows programs would have declined to a surmountable figure, perhaps 35,000.) Thus, the Department of Justice predicts the future of the computer business (and prosecutes Microsoft for interfering with the predictions) with as much confidence as the late Jeanne Dixon predicted the next year's headlines in the December issue of supermarket tabloids. One wonders what the DOJ has that will make its predictions any more reliable than Ms. Dixon's.

Technological Lock-in
and Path Dependence

The "applications barrier to entry" claim is an application of the broader theories of "path dependence" and "technological lock-in" popularized by economist Brian Arthur.[39] Path dependence began as an observation from natural history that events in the past can irrevocably foreclose future choices. If a particular species of turtles becomes extinct today, then there is no possibility the species could thrive ten thousand years later, even if the environment changed to become ideally suitable for that turtle species.

When this theory is applied to human-created tools, it is called "technological lock-in." If one type of technology becomes widespread at a certain time, the costs of switching might become so high that people will keep using the technology even when superior technologies are available.

As detailed above, the technological lock-in theory does not apply to PC operating systems, because the costs of switching are so low—as long as a new operating system ensures some form of compatibility with programs from the old operating system.

At a broader level, the technological lock-in theory does not properly account for the crucial difference between humans and turtles: Humans can consciously plan for their future and can direct the evolution of their technological tools. Turtles cannot plan the evolution of their species, and so what happens to turtles may be much more irrevocable than are the choices humans make about tools.

At a particular level, the case histories chosen to prove that technological lock-in exists turn out to be hokum, without exception. The most famous lock-in myth involves computer keyboards. From the early days of the typewriter, keyboards were arranged in the "QWERTY" pattern (named for the uppermost, leftmost row of letter keys). Decades later, a man named Dvorak proposed that typewriter keys be arranged alphabetically. By the late 1980s, the Dvorak keyboard had become the number one talking point for path dependence, based on assertions that studies showed the Dvorak keyboard was clearly superior for training time and typing speed.

Further inquiry, however, revealed that the studies demonstrating the superiority of the Dvorak keyboard were mostly conducted by Dvorak himself, involved small samples and questionable methods, and were contradicted by

---

[39]W. Brian Arthur, *Increasing Returns and Path Dependence in the Economy* (Ann Arbor, MI: University of Michigan Press, 1994).

other research.[40] The QWERTY keyboard arrangement had been chosen after experiments showed it produced fewer instances of typewriter keys colliding with each other. Once keys were replaced by typing balls (*e.g.*, on IBM Selectric typewriters) or computer keyboards, the original rationale became irrelevant, but QWERTY has remained in use because there is no evidence any other arrangement would be faster.

A second supposed example of path dependence involves the ascendance of the VHS standard for home videocassette players and recorders and the demise of the Betamax standard. Beta produced better picture quality, we are told, but because of some marketing fluke from the 1970s, we are all using the inferior VHS standard today, and nobody can switch because the number of VHS tapes and tape players is too large.

This is once again nonsense. Beta was introduced in April 1975; VHS was not available until the summer of 1977. Despite Beta's two-year lead, which created an installed base consisting entirely of Beta, VHS was able to catch up quickly—even though the theory of path dependence would suggest VHS's catch-up was impossible. VHS priced itself aggressively, so that Beta usually was catching up with VHS's price cuts. More importantly, the first version of VHS gave consumers what two years of Betamax had not: the ability to tape an entire movie on a single cassette. Beta tapes were only an hour long. Beta eventually brought out two-hour tapes, but by then VHS had four-hour tapes. VHS never allowed Beta to get cheaper than VHS, and VHS continued to offer superior recording times. What about the supposed technical superiority of Beta? Reviews in *Consumer Reports* do not support any claim that Betamax had superior picture quality.

Betamax is better for sophisticated editing work, which is why it is still used by many television stations. As for consumer uses, the VHS/Beta story *disproves* the theory that inferior products can sustain dominance simply because they were dominant at some earlier time.[41]

The world is full of popular inventions that the technological lock-in theory cannot explain. CD-ROM drives became popular on computers even though there was little software for them at first, whereas there was a great deal of software for floppy disk drives (an applications barrier to entry?). Compact disk players for music became popular, even though there was at first very little recorded music on CD, as opposed to vinyl or tape. A hundred years ago,

---

[40]Among many other irregularities, Dvorak used experienced typists on his own keyboard, while assigning the QWERTY keyboard to people who had scored a zero on previous typing tests. Stan J. Liebowitz and Stephen E. Margolis, *Winners, Losers & Microsoft, supra* note 27, pages 23-44.

[41]*Ibid.*, pages 120-127.

automobiles began to become popular—even though gasoline filling stations were difficult to find, and oats for horses were plentiful.

MICROSOFT OFFICE

During the Microsoft trial, the prosecutors did not allege and introduced no evidence suggesting Microsoft had a monopoly in any type of software application, including the bundled collections of business productivity programs called office suites. Microsoft is in this market with a product called Microsoft Office. Allegations based on Microsoft Office's market share had been made before trial by the state attorneys general who joined the lawsuit, but those allegations were never presented to the court for fact-finding.

Nevertheless, after all the evidence had been heard and the judge had made it clear he would entertain no new evidence, the government began claiming Microsoft had a monopoly over office suites, too. The government's proposal to break up Microsoft is explicitly premised on the "fact" that Office is a monopoly—even though there had been no such finding of fact, and Microsoft has never had the opportunity to contest this charge. Nevertheless, Judge Jackson ordered Microsoft Office to be divorced from Windows, with each put in a separate company.[42]

The programs that make up a typical office suite were usually sold separately in the 1980s, but by the late 1990s most companies were following Microsoft's innovation of putting several integrated programs into a single package priced much lower than the programs would cost separately. The two core programs for office suites are spreadsheets and word processing. Programs for email, presentations, databases, and Web site management are now often included. Usually a suite will have a basic version, and also more expensive versions that include databases or other extra programs.

The original "killer application" in the business world was the VisiCalc spreadsheet, later displaced by the much superior Lotus 1-2-3. Lotus was secure on top until the 1989 introduction of Microsoft Excel for Windows, ranked clearly superior by computer magazines. Lotus worsened its problems in the next few years by failing to bring out new versions of 1-2-3 for Windows and by dropping its version of 1-2-3 for Macintosh. It was this blunder that gave Microsoft the opportunity to sell the Microsoft Excel spreadsheet to many new

---

[42]*United States v. Microsoft, Final Judgment* [hereinafter, "Jackson Final Judgment"], ¶ 2.

customers.[43]

WordStar was the superior word processor of the early 1980s, allowing users to embed rich formatting. WordStar, though, failed to match the innovations of WordPerfect, the first word processing application that did not require users to switch between "text mode" (for typing words) and "command mode" (for entering formatting instructions). By the late 1980s, Microsoft's Word for DOS was about even with WordPerfect in computer magazine rankings. But unlike Excel, Word was not clearly superior to its competitors.

Fortunately for Microsoft, WordPerfect self-destructed. The company's popular policy of free telephone support was dropped. Windows 3.0 was introduced in 1989, but not until 1992 did WordPerfect produce a version for Windows, and that version was unstable, prone to inexplicable crashes, and bug-infested. Similarly, Windows 95 came out in August 1995, and most leading software manufacturers had Windows 95 products on store shelves by Christmas. WordPerfect, however, produced nothing until May 1996. Subsequent releases of WordPerfect usually managed to match most of the features of the previous release of Microsoft Word, but they were increasingly bug-ridden and prone to interfering with the rest of the computer. (Although I had been a loyal WordPerfect user since 1987 (version 4.2, for DOS), I finally gave up in the spring of 1999, when the installation routine failed to work on my business computer, but the install program did manage to destroy the user files from my speech recognition program.)

How much did Microsoft's primacy in the OS market help Office climb to the top of the office applications market? Perhaps not very much. Office has a large market share of Apple users. This can't be the result of Windows leveraging by Microsoft. Novell, on the other hand, was the leading networking manufacturer when it bought WordPerfect, hoping to exploit synergies between networking and office applications. But, as noted above, WordPerfect's quality declined greatly under Novell's ownership, while the networking software had its own problems meeting the competition.

In the market of financial management programs, Quicken by Intuit had 78 percent of retail consumer sales as of February 2000, while Microsoft Money had 18 percent.[44] Even though it distributes a free trial version of Money over the Internet, Microsoft has not been able to translate its OS leadership into even a close second in the financial management market.

In the office suite market, Microsoft has aggressively followed its standard

---

[43]Stan J. Liebowitz and Stephen E. Margolis, *Winners, Losers & Microsoft, supra* note 27, pages 178-179.

[44]Rob Kaiser, "Computer Users to Notice Ruling," *Chicago Tribune*, April 4, 2000.

policy of expanding market share through low-cost pricing. For example, while WordPerfect was the leading word processing program, prices for such programs rose 35 percent. Since Microsoft has become the leading supplier, prices have fallen 75 percent.[45] Prices for other office suite items (spreadsheets, presentation programs, medium-sized database programs) have fallen by similar amounts. Microsoft was, as noted above, the first company to start combining business productivity programs into an integrated suite, at a steep discount off the price of the separate programs.

Microsoft Office faces competition today, and it will likely face much more tomorrow. The history of the rise of Microsoft Office to its current strong position is evidence that a dominant position in a software market one day is no guarantee of continued dominance if the leading company fails to innovate and meet consumers' needs.

In February 2000, Microsoft Office accounted for 88 percent of office suites sold to consumers at retail. Corel (which owns WordPerfect and Quattro) had 11 percent, and IBM's Lotus Smart Suite had only 1 percent.[46]

While Microsoft has a very strong position in retail sales of office suites, the retail-only figure overlooks some strong competitors to Office. Sun Microsystems has started giving its Star Office suite away for free over the Internet. Forty thousand copies a day were being downloaded in October 1999.[47] Another company offers a full-featured suite for free at MyWebOS.com.

Giving products away has long been a way for competitors to erode a leader's market share, and the strategy works particularly well for software since distribution costs via the Internet are low. Another strategy is to allow consumers switching from one suite to another to buy the full product for the same price as an upgrade for existing users.

Many original equipment manufacturers (OEMs) pre-load suite software on their new computers. While Microsoft Office is popular in the OEM channel, IBM and Polywell pre-load the Lotus Smart Suite; Quantex and Cybermax load WordPerfect; and eMachines uses Star Office.

Office suites are also becoming available online, such as the Java-based ThinkFree Office, which touts its compatibility with Microsoft Office.[48] Visto Corp., of Mountain View, California, makes a suite of Web-based applications

---

[45]Stan Liebowitz, "Bill Gates' Secret? Better Products," *Wall Street Journal*, October 20, 1998, page A22.

[46] Rob Kaiser, "Computer Users to Notice Ruling," *supra* note 44.

[47]"Scott McNealy's Plan to Punish Bill Gates," *Fortune*, October 25, 1999. See also, Elinor Abrams, "Sun Takes Aim at Microsoft Office," *The Industry Standard*, July 31, 2000, page 73.

[48]www.thinkfree.com.

that duplicate the functions of Microsoft Office, and Magicaldesk.com offers the same.[49] Because these products are aimed at business users, many of whom already have high-speed Internet connections, rather than home users, most of whom still use dial-up modems, bandwidth constraints are less an issue.

Another approach to using the Web for marketing suites is to lease office software to businesses for a period of time. During the lease period, any upgrade or improvement is automatically delivered for free over the Internet. The new Microsoft.net and Oracle Business Online programs take this approach. For most businesses, the cost of hardware is minor compared to the costs of installing, maintaining, and upgrading software. If the model works, it can cut the ratio of computer administrators to computers.

In summary, the charge that Microsoft Office monopolizes the office suite market was never made or substantiated during the trial, yet emerged as part of Judge Jackson's decision to split up the company. The history of Microsoft Office shows a superior product winning market share on its merits, helped along by the missteps of some of its principal competitors. There is no evidence of monopoly power: Prices have been falling since Office became the market leader, and new competitors continue to enter the market.

MARKET SHARE and the BENEFITS OF STANDARDIZATION

In the IT industry, there is a clear trend toward standards-setting companies acquiring large market shares. Products with shares of more than 70 percent of their respective markets include Intel's microprocessors, Cisco's Internet routers, Qualcomm's digital cell phones, and Palm's personal digital assistants.[50]

Does this mean these companies are monopolists and potential targets for antitrust prosecution? Treasury Secretary Lawrence H. Summers thinks not. He commented recently that companies doing business in the Digital Economy often have

> very large fixed costs and much smaller marginal costs . . . [and] the only incentive to produce anything is the possession of temporary monopoly power; because without that power the price will be bid

---

[49]Stewart Alsop, "Go Ahead! Chuck Your PC Software," *Fortune*, May 10, 1999, page 149.

[50]Michael A. Cusumano, "The Some Fine Mess You've Made, Mr. Gates," *Wall Street Journal*, April 5, 2000.

down to marginal cost and the high initial fixed cost cannot be recouped. So constant pursuit of monopoly becomes the central driving thrust of the new economy. And the creative destruction that results from all that striving becomes the essential spur of economic growth.[51]

Whether or not one agrees with Summers, it is clear there can be important standardization benefits when one firm achieves a very large market share. For example, if software developers have one standard to work on, they can concentrate on improving their programs, rather than on having to write them many different ways for many different operating systems.[52]

The benefits to consumers may be even greater. One computer professional recalls the days before standardization, in the early 1980s:

> Every computer had its own operating system, and they were all pretty much incompatible in odd ways. It was insane. Finding software to do exactly what you wanted was incredibly frustrating. Software developers couldn't be expected to put out all these different versions of their work. As a result, you usually either paid a fortune for what you needed, or you went without. A common mantra was, "find the software to do what you want, then pick the hardware that will run it."

> There wasn't any $49.95 software. A sorting program cost $100. Word processing was $495, and did squat compared to what you get today. Database, $495. Spreadsheet, $495. Disk defragger, $100.

> You do *not* want to go back to the way it was before.[53]

Does this sound like we've moved from a competitive market to a monopolized market? Falling prices, rising quality, and expanding choices for consumers are all hallmarks of a competitive (and lightly regulated) marketplace, not its monopolized opposite.

---

[51]Lawrence Summers, "The Wealth of Nations," speech delivered on May 10, 2000, distributed by the U.S. Treasury Department.

[52]Barry Fagin, *The Case Against the Case Against Microsoft* (Washington, DC: Competitive Enterprise Institute, 1999), page 7.

[53]Win Schaeffer, "Microsoft's Merits," *Chicago Tribune*, November 10, 1999.

BRIEFLY STATED . . .

The Sherman Act's language is so vague that *any* business operating in America today could be targeted for prosecution no matter what business practices it engages in. By casting so wide a net, the Act gives politicians and government officials discretionary power over which companies to target, a power that thoughtful observers from Adam Smith and the Founding Fathers to many economists today would say is just the opposite of what is needed for an economy to operate efficiently.

The story of the rise of Microsoft Windows and Microsoft Office to their current positions of market leadership does not reveal the effects of an "applications barrier to entry," "path dependence," or any other non-market forces. Instead, it shows the steady application of Microsoft's high-volume/low-price strategy combined with continuous improvements to product quality and, in some cases, superior customer service.

Large market shares may be an inherent characteristic of the new Digital Economy, perhaps due in part to the difference in fixed costs and marginal costs noted by Lawrence Summers and in part to the role of e-commerce in allowing consumers to identify and choose superior products much more quickly and accurately than is the case with products and services in the Old Economy. Either way, there is little evidence that Microsoft has inordinate market power today or that consumers would be better off if Microsoft's competitors were somehow favored in the future.

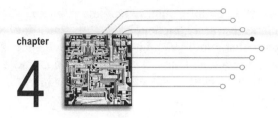

Ordinary
Business Practices

T his chapter examines some of the particular acts performed by Microsoft that allegedly violate the Sherman Antitrust Act. Internet Explorer issues will be covered separately in Chapter Five.

According to Representative Sherman himself, and according to Supreme Court interpretation of the Sherman Act, there is nothing wrong with gaining a monopoly through superior skill and a better product.[1] Justice Jackson's findings of fact acknowledged that Microsoft had done nothing wrong in achieving its Windows "monopoly."

As a company grows and wins market share, on the way to achieving monopoly, it will do things such as raise prices, lower prices, give products away for free, make reciprocal arrangements with other companies, and talk roughly about the competition. All of these practices are legal and help build market share.

Then, antitrust theory goes, the company becomes so successful that it achieves a monopoly. Suddenly, what were legal business practices become illegal. Conduct that helped the company satisfy consumers in the past is now

---

[1] A monopoly created "by growth or development as a consequence of superior product, business acumen, or historic accident" is not illegal. *United States v. Grinnell Corp.*, 384 U.S. 563 (1996).

labeled "anti-competitive" and grounds for litigation and substantial punishment.

It would be bad enough if antitrust simply outlawed ordinary business practices when those practices come from a "monopolist." But since the company does not learn it is a "monopolist" until years later—when the Justice Department's Antitrust Division or the Federal Trade Commission brings and wins a case in court—the company has no practical way of knowing whether its ordinary business practices are lawful or not.

WINDOWS PRICING

Real monopolists charge high prices because they do not need to worry about competition. The inflation-adjusted retail price of Windows has fallen some 50 percent over the last decade.[2] The Windows operating system of today includes vastly more features than its predecessors. Are declining prices and increasing output the characteristics of a monopoly?

If Microsoft Windows were essential for the operation of personal computers, and if there were no long-term threat of competition, then Microsoft would, rationally, charge between $900 and $2,000 for each copy of Windows, explained MIT economist Richard Schmalensee during the trial.[3] This would nearly double the price of a personal computer, so some people just wouldn't buy PCs. But others who must have computers for work or other necessary projects would, presumably, pay the higher price. Microsoft would sell fewer copies of Windows but make a much larger profit on each one, presumably (once again) earning greater net profits in the process. That would be classic monopoly conduct: raising prices and reducing output.

But in the real world, if Microsoft tried to set Windows prices that high, Windows computers would lose their price advantage over Apple computers. Recall from the earlier discussion that it was Microsoft's *lower* prices that originally enticed buyers into the Intel-Microsoft camp in the 1990s. Many people would react to the higher prices by switching to Apple. Others would make the extra effort to learn Linux. And the first company to invent an easy-to-use operating system compatible with Windows could sell its new OS for $600 a copy!

---

[2]Richard B. McKenzie, *Trust on Trial: How the Microsoft Case is Reframing the Rules of Competition* (Cambridge, MA: Perseus Books, 2000), pages 40, 42-43.

[3]For more, see Bernard J. Reddy, David S. Evans, and Albert L. Nichols, *Why Does Microsoft Charge So Little for Windows?* (Cambridge, MA: National Economic Research Associates, January 7, 1999).

The price of personal computer operating systems today looks much like what one might expect if the products were in competition with each other. In a retail computer store in 1999, the Windows 98 upgrade was $89, IBM's OS/2 was $100, Apple's MacOS 8.0 was $85, and Red Hat's Linux 6.0 was $80. The odd one out is Sun Solaris, at $430.[4] Which seems more indicative of a monopoly price being extracted from some narrowly defined market: the $89 price or the $430 price? It says a lot about antitrust that the company charging $430 managed to convince the Antitrust Division that the company charging $89 was the one charging monopoly prices.

In real, inflation-adjusted dollars, the retail consumer price for a virgin installation of Windows rose 10 percent over the last decade. The price of a Windows upgrade from a previous version fell 46 percent.[5] In order to add to Windows 3.0 all the features now included in Windows 98 or Windows ME by buying each program individually, one would have had to spend several hundred dollars; in terms of utility per dollar, the price of Windows has fallen substantially.

Also, examining the price of Windows alone overlooks the fact that when Windows 3.0 was introduced in April 1990, it was not a complete operating system. Windows had to run on top of DOS. The two products together cost $205. When Windows 98 was introduced, the program was self-sufficient (no DOS required) and cost $169 (or $89 for an upgrade from earlier versions of Windows).[6]

Windows Pricing to Computer Manufacturers

If Windows were a monopoly, a decade of falling prices would not be the only pricing fact difficult to explain. A consumer typically pays $179 for a new version of Windows or $89 for an upgrade. A computer manufacturer, or OEM (original equipment manufacturer), spends less, about $40-$50 for a new version of Windows. Part of the price difference is a volume discount, since the OEM is buying many copies at once, while the consumer only one. Also,

---

[4]Richard B. McKenzie, *Trust on Trial*, *supra* note 2, page 41.

[5]Barry Fagin, *The Case Against the Case Against Microsoft* (Washington, DC: Competitive Enterprise Institute, 1999), page 15, Figure 3.

[6]Stan Liebowitz, "A Defective Product: Consumer Groups' Study of Microsoft in Need of Recall" (Washington, DC: Competitive Enterprise Institute, February 9, 1999), page 3.

computer manufacturers provide Windows technical support to their customers, whereas Microsoft incurs the cost of technical support for consumer versions sold at retail.

Even so, the price of Windows to OEMs is inexplicable if Microsoft is a monopoly. Whereas a consumer faced with a Microsoft monopoly always has the choice not to buy—he can just keep using the old version of Windows or buy an Apple Computer instead—the OEMs have no such flexibility. Customers expect that a new computer from a company like Gateway or Dell will include the latest version of Windows, not a version from a few years ago. And Gateway and Dell do not have the option of selling Apple computers instead of Intel-type computers. Therefore, Microsoft, as a profit-maximizing monopolist, ought to make prices *especially* high for the captive OEMs. As a monopolist, Microsoft ought to be able to *at least* raise the price of Windows by an order of magnitude, to around $400-$500 (much higher than the $179 consumer price). Computer manufacturers would pass the price increase on to consumers, and computer sales would drop some. But even if computer sales fell by half (very unlikely), Microsoft would be making 10 times as much per unit and thus quintupling its profit from OEM sales.

As will be discussed below, Microsoft does earn "follow-on" profits by selling applications (particularly, Office) to users who have bought the Windows operating system, so even if Windows were given away free, there would be some profits earned via the sale of these follow-on products. However, the follow-on profits from applications are not so large as to account for the full difference between Windows' actual OEM price and the theoretical monopoly price.[7]

At trial, the government's economists were unable to offer any credible explanation for Windows pricing to OEMs. Franklin Fisher, one of the government's economists testifying during the trial, said Microsoft was earning its monopoly profits "elsewhere."[8] He couldn't specify where the "elsewhere" was, but he knew Microsoft was a very profitable company.

The other government economist, Dr. Frederick Warren-Boulton, acknowledged that Microsoft Windows was priced low currently, but warned Microsoft might raise the price to monopoly levels in the future.[9] Yet within the narrow market defined by the DOJ—Intel-compatible personal computers—

---

[7]Bernard J. Reddy, David S. Evans, and Albert L. Nichols, *Why Does Microsoft Charge So Little for Windows? supra* note 3, pages 7-9.

[8]Richard B. McKenzie, *Trust on Trial, supra* note 2, page 32.

[9]*Ibid.*

Microsoft has had a 90 percent market share for years and has not raised prices. What makes Dr. Warren-Boulton believe Microsoft will abandon its low-price/high-volume strategy in the future, and that the government must protect consumers from the threat that Microsoft might abruptly change the business strategy the company has used since its founding?

The only plausible explanation for Microsoft's OEM pricing is that Microsoft realizes it is threatened with competition, and prices its software accordingly. Should Microsoft attempt to extract monopoly profits from OEMs, more OEMs would shift to Linux. Even more threatening to Microsoft would be the likelihood of new OS entrants.

Intel, for example, could integrate a new Intel OS with its chips. Since Windows needs to be compatible with other chips, such as those from AMD and Cyrix, an Intel chip with a built-in OS would probably perform better than Windows running on an Intel chip. Intel has massive market capitalization, giving it the financial resources to go toe-to-toe with Microsoft in a long-term battle for operating system dominance. If Intel could make money selling an operating system to OEMs for, say, $150 each, then Intel, as a profit-maximizing corporation, should be in the OS business.

That scenario is not entirely hypothetical. Before the introduction of Windows 95, Intel was developing "Native Signal Processing," which would have had the Intel chip perform certain multimedia functions, such as audio playback, rather than having the function performed by Windows.[10] Microsoft successfully discouraged Intel from pursuing that project. Judge Jackson found Microsoft's action had no pro-competitive justification, but the justification is quite obvious. NSP would be only for Intel chips, which would disadvantage other companies that make chips for PCs that run Windows. Microsoft would be forced to build different versions of Windows for Intel chips and other chips.

The reason Intel is not in the OS market—and the reason other companies, such as Sun or AOL/Netscape, also are not—is that Microsoft prices Windows low to keep potential competitors out. If Microsoft has a monopoly, it is sustained by unusually *low* prices, and there is no evidence Microsoft ever will or could raise its prices to take advantage of its dominant market share. This situation is obviously beneficial to consumers. The only people who are harmed (and the word must be used loosely) are Microsoft's competitors, who are kept from charging higher prices and earning bigger profits, and those Microsoft stockholders who care more about quarterly profits than long-run investment returns.

---

[10]David S. Evans and Richard L. Schmalensee, "The Economics of the Microsoft Antitrust Case: A Post-Trial Primer," presentation to the AEI-Brookings Center on Regulatory Policy (Washington, DC: February 11, 2000), http://www.neramicrosoft.com (National Economic Research Associates), pages 129-130, note 92.

GOVERNMENT'S RESPONSE

Faced with these facts, the DOJ and Microsoft's competitors offer a litany of specious reasons why Microsoft must still be considered a monopolist. First, Robert Bork claims Microsoft's market share and profitability prove it is a monopolist. Never mind that Bork's classic book, *The Antitrust Paradox*, vigorously denounces reliance on market share or profitability as proof of monopoly.[11] It is fair to say that this position represents (or at least represented, until recently) the consensus view of economists.[12]

A more sophisticated take on the DOJ's argument goes like this: A monopoly exists when there are insurmountable barriers to entry. It is true that other companies could make products that compete with Microsoft's, but in the past when the other companies did so, Microsoft lowered its prices to near zero, forcing competitors to match that price and not make any profit, and then to drop out of the market. Microsoft could do so because the marginal cost of producing an additional copy of software is near zero. Therefore, there is an insurmountable barrier to entry, and Microsoft is a monopolist.

This argument is a variation on the theory of predatory pricing, which we will return to in the following chapter on the "browser wars." At this point, it should be sufficient to point out that the marginal cost of producing one extra copy of Windows *is* near zero, but the marginal cost of another Windows sale is not.[13] Getting more customers requires more advertising and marketing expenses. The marginal customers are, by definition, those who are less interested in computers in general, or Windows in particular, rather than the customers who have already bought. Thus, marketing and advertising costs rise at the margin. In addition, each new Windows customer requires technical support (supplied by Microsoft for retail sales or by the OEM for OEM sales); marginal customers, being less sophisticated about computers, might be expected to cause rising marginal technical support costs. Thus, computer software may not be something new in the world of economics after all. More

---

[11]Robert H. Bork, *The Antitrust Paradox: A Policy at War with Itself* (New York, NY: Basic Books, 1978).

[12]Richard A. Posner, *Natural Monopoly and Its Regulation* (Washington, DC: Cato Institute, 1999 [1969]); Franklin M. Fisher and John L. McGowan, "On the Misuse of Accounting Rates of Return to Infer Monopoly Profits," 73 *American Economic Review* 82-97 (1983); S.C. Littlechild, "Misleading Calculations of Social Costs of Monopoly Power," 91 *Economic Journal* 348-363 (1981); Harold Demsetz, "Industry Structure, Market Rivalry, and Public Policy," 16 *Journal of Law and Economics* 1 (1973). For a critical review of recent departures from this consensus, see Fred S. McChesney and William F. Shughart II, editors, *The Causes and Consequences of Antitrust: The Public-Choice Perspective* (Chicago, IL: University of Chicago Press, 1995), pages 341-349.

[13]Stan J. Liebowitz and Stephen E. Margolis, *Winners, Losers & Microsoft* (Oakland, CA: Independent Institute, 1999), pages 8-9.

likely, it is just another industry of many, such as book publishing or television broadcasting, with high initial fixed costs and relatively low marginal costs.

APPLICATIONS PRICING

Trends in the inflation-adjusted retail prices of Microsoft's application products between 1990 and 1999 do not resemble what would be expected from a monopolist. The retail price of Excel is down 29 percent; an Excel upgrade, down 77 percent; Word, up 7 percent; and a Word upgrade, down 73 percent.[14] The entire Office suite—with a very powerful word processing program, spreadsheet program, presentations program, and email program—costs less to buy in 1999 than the leading stand-alone word processing program did in 1980.[15]

In markets where Microsoft is not present, software prices have declined about 15 percent; in markets Microsoft enters, prices have declined an average of 60 percent.[16]

That Microsoft follows a high-volume/low-price strategy does not mean the company never raises prices to any customer for any product. Although prices are far below monopoly levels, Microsoft has raised Windows and Office prices somewhat for some OEMs and large businesses in the past few years. Microsoft recently eliminated one form of licensing for Office: Instead of paying according to the number of people using Office at one time, businesses will have to pay based on the number of computers that run Office. Per-unit costs will be lower, but total costs will be higher.[17]

That a company raises prices to some customers, while cutting prices to others does not prove it has a monopoly. More likely, the company is doing a better job of estimating marginal demand in different sub-markets—just as airlines have learned to raise prices for business travelers (who must travel), while cutting prices for vacationers (who have more discretion about departure and arrival times and destinations).

It is interesting to contrast Microsoft's pricing strategy with Apple's. Apple makes the MacOS, the only OS that works on Apple computers, for which

---

[14] Barry Fagin, *The Case Against the Case Against Microsoft*, *supra* note 5.

[15] *Ibid.*

[16] Stan J. Liebowitz and Stephen E. Margolis, *Winners, Losers & Microsoft*, *supra* note 13, pages 194-257.

[17] Amy Cortese, "There's More than One Way to Play Monopoly," *Business Week*, January 26, 1998, page 36.

Apple has a patented monopoly. For most of the last two decades, Apple has not licensed to other manufacturers the authority to make Apple-compatible machines. Thus, the MacOS and Macintosh hardware are bound by a "tying arrangement," a candidate for antitrust prosecution if Apple had gained larger market share. The fact that Apple's pricing strategy did not work may explain why it is not being sued today for being a monopolist.

The real history of Apple illustrates how the economics of the Digital Economy work strongly against attempts to wring too much profit out of products over the long term. The market capitalization for high-price/low-volume Apple was $5 billion when this was written, whereas it is $400 billion for high-volume/low-price Microsoft.

RECIPROCAL ARRANGEMENTS WITH OEMS

IBM helped Microsoft develop Windows 3.1 in return for a special discount from Microsoft for later purchases of the program. Compaq helped develop Windows 95 and similarly received preferential treatment. Such discounts are an ordinary practice between businesses for obvious reasons: A special discount is a reasonable reward for a company that contributes to the design of a new product. For Microsoft, developing a new operating system was made easier by working with major OEMs on whose hardware the software would eventually run. The partnerships plainly benefitted consumers by producing operating systems that were more robust, less buggy, and better tested before their release.

In the topsy-turvy world of antitrust law, though, Microsoft's reciprocal relationships with computer manufacturers constituted preferential discounts and hence were illegal acts. During the antitrust trial, IBM complained it didn't get the same deal on Windows 95 that Compaq did . . . even though IBM did nothing to help with the design or testing of Windows 95, and only belatedly decided to license Windows 95 when it discovered its own OS/2 wasn't very popular.

Under the terms of Judge Jackson's order breaking up Microsoft, the company would be forbidden to offer special discounts to companies that help it develop better products. The inevitable result would be more bugs, fewer advanced features, and higher prices for consumers. Somehow, this isn't what most observers would expect to be the result of government acting in the "public interest."

Microsoft also gives discounts to OEMs whose new machines include hardware that takes advantage of Windows. For example, Windows 98 included support for the Universal Serial Bus—a socket in the back of the computer that makes it easier for consumers to attach peripherals (*e.g.*, a zip drive) to their computers than by using a serial or parallel port. OEMs that include a Universal Serial Bus get a discount on Windows.[18] The trial court's order in the Microsoft case, if upheld on appeal, would forbid such discounts.

VIOLATING THE ANTITRUST SPEECH CODE

During the trial, Microsoft was beaten up in the media when internal emails were discovered describing several employees' desires to extinguish the company's competitors. One of the most famous of these emails was about convincing Intel not to do business with Netscape: "[T]his strategy would cut off Netscape's air supply, keep them from gaining any revenue to invest in their business."[19]

Reports of the use of this phrase by Microsoft employees greatly outnumbered reports that Microsoft employees did not originate this macho phrase, but had *copied it* from employees at Oracle, the database giant, who were blustering about what Oracle would do to its much smaller rival, Informix.[20] Oracle, ironically, is one of the principal companies that lobbied for government action against Microsoft.[21] Despite the strong language, Netscape and Informix are both still breathing: Netscape was acquired by AOL for $4.3 billion, and Informix remains in business.

Another of the companies that incited the Microsoft case was AOL . . . and the irony continues. The company's "AOL Anywhere" slogan highlights the company's ambition for an overwhelming share of every Internet access market—televisions, smart phones, pagers, computers with narrowband or broadband, and anything else that might be invented. Microsoft used to have a similar slogan, "Windows Everywhere," emphasizing the company's ambition to spread the use of computers and establish Windows as the operating system for those computers.

---

[18]"Meet Microsoft's Enforcer," *Business Week*, November 30, 1998, page 136.

[19]Quoted in Franklin M. Fisher and Daniel L. Rubinfeld, "*United States v. Microsoft*: An Economic Analysis," in David S. Evans, Franklin M. Fisher, Daniel L. Rubinfeld, and Richard L. Schmalensee, *Did Microsoft Harm Consumers? Two Opposing Views* (Washington, DC: AEI-Brookings Joint Center for Regulatory Studies, 2000), page 19.

[20]"Does Everyone Do It?" *Business Week*, November 2, 1998, page 30.

[21]Even more ironic is Oracle CEO Larry Ellison's recent boast: "In fact, we dominate. We almost have a Gates-like share in the Internet, and it's the Internet that's driving the business." Quoted in Richard B. McKenzie, *Trust on Trial*, *supra* note 2, page 55.

Unlike AOL and the Microsoft of yore, Cisco Systems Inc. (which has a Microsoft-like market share for Internet routers) warns its employees not to use strong language. Its salespeople are trained to avoid phrases such as "kill the competition" or "dominate the market."[22] Cisco's style of self-censorship appears to be one consequence of antitrust laws. Antitrust lawyers are warning their clients not to use politically incorrect "war words," such as "dominance," or words based on sports analogies.[23]

A CONTRACT DISPUTE OVER JAVA

Java is a computer programming language invented by Sun Microsystems in the mid-1990s. Java's promise is "write once, read anywhere." If a computer programmer writes in Java, then Java will allow the program to run on any type of operating system, including Sun Solaris, Linux, other Unix flavors, Windows, and MacOS.

Java is therefore a form of "middleware"—a kind of software that mediates between the application program and the operating system. Windows versions 1.0 through 3.1 were also middleware; they mediated between the application program and the underlying operating system (DOS). Windows 95 and 98, by contrast, are pure operating systems; nothing stands in between them and the computer hardware. Another form of middleware is HTML (Hypertext Markup Language), the universal language of the World Wide Web. When a Web site designer writes a Web page in HTML, he knows the consumer's HTML browser will take care of displaying the page on the computer monitor; the Web site writer does not need to worry about what operating systems the consumers are running.

As the above examples show, middleware can be platform-specific (Windows 3.1 could run only on DOS) or cross-platform (Java and HTML).

When Sun introduced Java, the company worked hard to convince operating system companies, such as Microsoft, to build Java support into their future operating systems. When the OS companies agreed to do so, as Microsoft did, they signed contracts with Java giving the OS companies various rights concerning using Java logos, touting Java compatibility, and so forth. In exchange, the OS companies agreed to meet standards for implementing Java.

Windows creates "virtual machines" (a set of software routines, not physical

---

[22]Scott Thurm, "Microsoft's Behavior is Helping Cisco Learn How to Avoid Trouble," *Wall Street Journal*, June 1, 2000.

[23]"The Order's Impact on Industry, Law and the Economy," *Wall Street Journal*, June 8, 2000, page A10.

machines) to run programs written for certain non-Windows operating systems, such as Java or DOS. From the consumer's point of view, the Java Virtual Machine is invisible; from the operating system's point of view, the Virtual Machine helps the non-Windows program communicate with the Windows OS. For "pure" Java programs (not written for any particular OS platform), Microsoft's Java Virtual Machine performed *better* than Sun's own Solaris operating system, according to computer magazine tests.[24] According to Microsoft's view of the Sun/Microsoft contract, Microsoft has exceeded its contractual obligations.

Microsoft also added features to Windows allowing Windows users to take advantage of Java programs written specifically for Windows. By providing special features for Windows-specific Java, Microsoft thereby encouraged developers to write Windows-specific Java, rather than neutral Java. Note this did not prevent Microsoft's Java Virtual Machine from outperforming other OSs for developers who preferred to write pure cross-platform Java.

Sun brought suit against Microsoft, claiming Microsoft's creation of Windows-specific enhancements for Java violated Sun's copyright on Java and the Sun/Microsoft licensing agreement. The copyright claim was dismissed in May 2000, a victory for Microsoft, while Sun won a preliminary injunction requiring Microsoft to modify its Java Virtual Machine so Java programs can use Sun's method (rather than Microsoft's preferred method) for accessing the Windows APIs.[25] Meanwhile, the contract claim is proceeding to trial.

The Sun/Microsoft dispute about the contract terms of the Java licensing agreement is a fairly routine business-to-business dispute that can be resolved under ordinary contract law, with no need for recourse to the uncertain world of antitrust. Nevertheless, the Sun/Microsoft contract argument was turned into an antitrust claim against Microsoft when Judge Jackson found Microsoft had tried to "split" Java, *i.e.*, create its own proprietary version of the programming language. Yet if what Microsoft did constitutes a prohibited activity under the terms of the contract, then a court can order Microsoft to comply with the contract and pay appropriate damages for breach of contract.

Why should the Department of Justice care about a contract dispute between two companies that can afford their own lawyers? Because under the DOJ's theory of the Microsoft case, Microsoft attempted to stop Java from developing into middleware. The DOJ theory is fallacious in multiple ways. First, if Sun's

---

[24]David S. Evans and Richard L. Schmalensee, "The Economics of the Microsoft Antitrust Case: A Post-Trial Primer," *supra* note 10, pages 59-60.

[25]David P. Hamilton, "Judge Dismisses One of Sun's Claims Against Microsoft," *Wall Street Journal,* May 10, 2000, page B12.

license with Microsoft *allowed* Microsoft to develop an improved Java for Windows—even if Sun later regretted the agreement, or if Sun's lawyers drafted the original agreement poorly—Microsoft's actions can hardly be determined to be anti-competitive.

Second, if Microsoft is found to have breached its contract with Sun, remember that Microsoft still produced the *best* Java Virtual Machine for *pure* (non-Windows-specific) Java programming. How can the company that produces the best operating system for pure Java stand convicted of violating antitrust laws by subverting pure Java?

The reason that Java has not turned into a major applications platform has nothing to do with Microsoft and everything to do with the inherent limitations of middleware. When software is customized for particular environments (*e.g.*, MacOS is customized for Motorola chips, and Windows OS is customized for Intel and Intel-compatible chips), the operating system can use specific routines that maximize power and speed. Similarly, an application customized for a particular OS can share those power and speed advantages.

Conversely, when software is written to run on *any* OS (Windows, Mac, Linux, all the Unix variants, BeOS, *etc.*), it typically must sacrifice speed, power, and/or performance. An analogy can be made to another artificially created "universal language," Esperanto.[26] Had Esperanto become universally popular, a person traveling to France, Germany, or the United States would need to speak only a single language. But even if France, Germany, and the United States had millions of people who could speak Esperanto as a second language, it is unlikely that many of the best philosophers, poets, and other deep thinkers would choose Esperanto as their primary language, since it would not allow them to communicate their ideas with the richness, nuance, detail, and complexity of their native languages. Like a native language, computer applications written for one OS contain countless adaptations and modifications taking into account the needs and opportunities specific to that OS.

Java, like other middleware, is the Esperanto of the computer world. Understood everywhere, it is not very useful for complex tasks anywhere. Java works adequately for a variety of simple tasks, such as Web "applets." For example, the ESPN Web site includes a Java applet that lets users enter the name of a baseball pitcher and a batter; the applet then queries a database and displays statistics about that particular pitcher/hitter match-up.

Whether Java will ever develop beyond minor-league uses remains to be seen. It is certainly not Microsoft's fault that Java has failed to do so yet. As Chris Hall, a software developer, and Robert Hall, a prominent economist based

---

[26]For more on Esperanto, see http://www.esperanto.net/info/index_en.html.

at the Hoover Institution, wrote in early 1999:

> It is interesting to see how much discussion of Microsoft has changed over the eight months since the government filed the case. In May 1998, Java was the center of attention in discussions of the possible displacement of Microsoft. Though Java is alive and well, today's threat to Windows is not Java but Linux. The most sensitive policy issue today is probably not the protection of Java from Microsoft's efforts to hobble rivals, but the protection of Linux. After all, Linux is a real operating system, capable of running all the major applications that drive the demand for Windows. Currently Java is being used successfully to create Web site applets and middleware, not as a desktop personal computer operating system. The threat to Windows from Java is still completely theoretical.[27]

Scott McNealy, head of Sun Microsystems and owner of Java, has energetically promoted the DOJ suit against Microsoft. He once claimed the only thing better than owning Windows would be owning English.[28] If we buy this metaphor, which we shouldn't,[29] then McNealy is like the man who invented Esperanto—a universal language with high theoretical appeal but much less practical utility than the inventor hoped. There is an important difference, however, between McNealy and Dr. L.L. Zamenhof, the man who invented Esperanto in 1887: Zamenhof never tried to use the coercive power of government against his rivals.

BRIEFLY STATED . . .

In sum, the business practices defined as anti-competitive by the Department of Justice in its antitrust suit against Microsoft turn out, on closer inspection, to be nothing more than ordinary business practices. In 1986, the Seventh Circuit Court of Appeals wrote,

---

[27]Chris E. Hall and Robert E. Hall, *National Policy on Microsoft: A Neutral Perspective* (version 2.0, 1999), page 55, www.NetEcon.com.

[28]"The only thing I'd rather own than Windows is English or Chinese or Spanish, because then I could charge you $249 for the right to speak English . . . . " "In Their Own Words: Three High-Tech CEOs Testify," *Wall Street Journal*, March 4, 1998.

[29]The obvious difference between Windows and English is that no one invented English. By contrast, Windows is intellectual property invented and refined by computer programmers working for Microsoft.

Opinion about the offense of monopolization has undergone an evolution. Forty years ago it was thought that even a firm with a lawful monopoly . . . could not be allowed to defend its monopoly against would-be competitors by tactics otherwise legitimate; it had to exercise special restraint—perhaps, indeed, had to hold its prices high, to encourage new entry. So Alcoa was condemned as a monopolist because it had assiduously created enough productive capacity to supply all new increments of demand for aluminum. . . . Later, as the emphasis of antitrust policy shifted from the protection of competition as a process of rivalry to the protection of competition as a means of promoting economic efficiency, it became recognized that the lawful monopolist should be free to compete like everyone else: otherwise the antitrust laws would be holding an umbrella over inefficient competitors.[30]

The Microsoft case reverts antitrust law to the standards of the 1940s, when companies with large market shares were forbidden to harm competitors through normal business practices.

Microsoft has not priced Windows or its applications in the fashion of a monopolist, but rather as a company knowing it has powerful competitors ready to enter the market unless prices are kept low and quality high. Its practice of giving discounts to computer manufacturers who help develop new versions of Windows, include hardware to take full advantage of Windows, and promote the Windows name is a standard practice in other industries that works to the benefit of consumers.

That the antitrust trial court found discounts, aggressive language in internal emails, and a contract disagreement to be evidence of antitrust violations shows how easily antitrust laws can be manipulated against almost any company—even a company whose success depends on continuously improving its products and lowering its prices.

---

[30]*Olympia Equip. Leasing Corp. v. Western Union Tel. Co.*, 797 F.2d 370, 375 (7th Cir., 1986) (citations omitted).

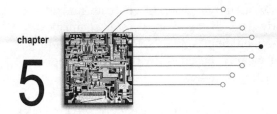

5

Internet Explorer vs. Netscape

A major part of the Microsoft case involves competition between the Netscape Web browser and Microsoft's Internet Explorer (IE) browser. This chapter begins by detailing how Netscape gained a browser monopoly, squandered it, and then regained the lead. Next, Netscape's putative role as a middleware platform is discussed, followed by an analysis of the ways in which Microsoft's competition with Netscape is claimed by the DOJ to have been anti-competitive. Particular attention is paid to Microsoft's integration of IE into the Windows operating system.

THE (TEMPORARY) MONOPOLIST

Some kinds of software, such as complex business databases (Oracle's specialty) or operating systems meant to run a wide variety of programs on many different computers (Microsoft's specialty) are very difficult to write. Internet browsers, by contrast, are not. As Chris Hall and Robert Hall explain:

. . . the browser is not a complex application and never did cost very much. The cost of developing a browser is not high. Mosaic—the predecessor of Netscape—was written by a group of graduate students in their spare time. In the early days of the Web, several companies developed their own browsers, including Apple, NetCom, and AOL, but they stopped development when it became obvious how cheaply they could license one of the existing browsers.[1]

A soon-to-be-famous Marc Andreeson and some other recent college graduates wrote the Netscape Navigator 1.0 Web browser in a few months. The browser bore many similarities to the Mosaic browser, created by the University of Illinois computing center, where Andreeson had been a student. Using tactics that clearly foreshadow those that would lead to Microsoft being accused of attempting to monopolize the browser market, Netscape distributed Navigator *en masse* for free and even took to calling its product the "Mosaic killer." Navigator was better than Mosaic, and it was free, so Mosaic sales plunged. Netscape found itself with a market share of 90 percent in 1994, a position it held until 1996.[2]

According to the antitrust model of "predatory pricing," once a company has destroyed its competitors with low prices (or in this case, by giving the product away for free), it can then raise prices to recoup its earlier losses. That is precisely what Netscape did. With Mosaic out of the way, Netscape began charging $49 for Navigator.[3]

By 1997, Netscape had lost its monopoly by charging excessive prices and failing to innovate. The company took much too long to respond to Microsoft's price competition. Although Microsoft started giving away IE for free in December 1995, Netscape kept its $49 price until 1997, then implemented a price cut of only $10 and did not resume offering the product for free until 1998.[4]

For a period of three years (more than a decade in Internet Time), Netscape not only had a monopoly over the browser market, but it also raised prices and

---

[1]Chris E. Hall and Robert E. Hall, *National Policy on Microsoft: A Neutral Perspective* (version 2.0, 1999), page 66, www.NetEcon.com.

[2]David Bank and John R. Wilke, "Microsoft and Justice End a Skirmish, Yet War Could Escalate," *Wall Street Journal*, November 25, 1998, page A1.

[3]Richard B. McKenzie, *Trust on Trial: How the Microsoft Case is Reframing the Rules of Competition* (Cambridge, MA: Perseus Books, 2000), page 89; Heather Green, "Has Netscape Hit the 'Innovation Ceiling'?" *Business Week*, January 19, 1998, page 69; "Play Nicely, or Not at All," *The Economist*, May 23, 1998, page 22.

[4]Richard B. McKenzie, *Trust on Trial*, ibid.

neglected the quality of its product in exactly the fashion one would expect from a monopolist. Antitrust theory tells us that monopolists often try to leverage their monopoly in one market to take over another market. One method for such leverage is "tying" or "bundling" the monopoly product with a product in the new market. During Netscape's monopoly period, Netscape began tying an email program to its browser, thus uniting two products for which the markets had formerly been separate. This bundling nearly destroyed Eudora, which had been the leading vendor of stand-alone email software.[5]

In late 1997, when Microsoft's challenge to Netscape's market share was becoming serious, Netscape head James Barksdale complained, "All I want is my God-given 90 percent market share."[6] Barksdale later insisted he was joking, but one can be sure that if Bill Gates had ever made a similar joke about a 90 percent market share, it would have been highly publicized evidence at the antitrust trial.

Barksdale's statement reflects his expectation that the Netscape monopoly would, or perhaps should, continue forever. This is certainly contrary to his view of Microsoft's alleged monopoly, which he expressed in testimony to the Senate Judiciary Committee in 1998:

> I was struck by the fact, in the response of Mr. Gates to the question about whether or not he was a monopoly, he talked about how short-lived the products were, and we all understand that. That doesn't negate whether or not it's a monopoly though. Even if it went away six months from now, it is a monopoly today.[7]

The Department of Justice alleges that once Microsoft set its sights on the browser market, Netscape was prevented from effectively distributing its Navigator browser. Yet in 1997, the number of Netscape users rose from 40 million to 65 million.[8] In mid-1998, Microsoft introduced Windows 98, which thoroughly integrated the Microsoft browser into the operating system. *Business Week* predicted: "Because Microsoft has woven browsing into Windows 98, due in June, it is practically assured of owning that market."[9]

---

[5]Clyde Wayne Crews, "Micro-Managing Bill Gates," *Washington Times*, March 2, 1998, page A19.

[6]Barbara Darrow, "James Barksdale," *Computer Reseller News*, November 17, 1997.

[7]"In Their Own Words: Three High-Tech CEOs Testify," *Wall Street Journal*, March 4, 1998.

[8]Susan Garland, "Nailing Microsoft Means Proving Harm Was Done," *Business Week*, November 16, 1998.

[9]"Justice Slows the Giant with 'Surgical Strikes'," *Business Week*, April 20, 1998, page 118.

As of mid-1998, though, *after* the DOJ launched its lawsuit alleging that Microsoft was attempting to "monopolize" the browser market, Microsoft had reached only parity with Netscape. By the end of the trial in late 1999, Microsoft was ahead, but far from achieving the dominance Netscape had once enjoyed: Microsoft had 56 percent and Netscape 40 percent.[10] Even when Netscape was losing market share to Microsoft, Netscape's user base was soaring, from 15 million in 1996 to 35 million in 1998, and perhaps doubling since the start of the Microsoft trial.[11] To the extent that Microsoft's aggressive promotion of Internet Explorer helped grow the number of people interested in the Internet—as even Judge Jackson acknowledged[12]—then Netscape gained many more potential customers, who were only a few mouse clicks away from the Netscape Netcenter.

The most important source of Microsoft's gain in market share was America Online's decision to use Internet Explorer as the AOL-branded browser. During the trial, America Online bought Netscape. Upon the expiration of the AOL/Microsoft contract in January 2001, AOL will switch its 25 million customers over to the Netscape browser. After the switch, Netscape will end (for now) the browser war where it began: in first place.

A few weeks before AOL announced it would switch to Netscape, the government's chief economic witnesses against Microsoft, Franklin Fisher and Daniel Rubinfeld, predicted AOL would *not* switch to Netscape: "[N]either economic analysis nor the actions and statements of AOL suggest that AOL will abandon IE for Navigator."[13] It is on the credibility of *these* economists—whose confident assertions about the future of the browser market have not survived even three months of Standard Time—that Microsoft stands condemned of

---

[10]David S. Evans and Richard L. Schmalensee, "The Economics of the Microsoft Antitrust Case: A Post-Trial Primer," presentation to the AEI-Brookings Center on Regulatory Policy (Washington, DC: February 11, 2000), http://www.neramicrosoft.com (National Economic Research Associates).

[11]Richard McKenzie, "Microsoft's 'Applications Barrier to Entry': The Missing 70,000 Programs," *Policy Analysis* No. 380 (Washington, DC: Cato Institute, 2000), pages 36-37.

[12]Jackson Findings of Fact, ¶ 408.

[13]Franklin M. Fisher and Daniel L. Rubinfeld, "*United States v. Microsoft*: An Economic Analysis," in David S. Evans, Franklin M. Fisher, Daniel L. Rubinfeld, and Richard L. Schmalensee, *Did Microsoft Harm Consumers? Two Opposing Views* (Washington, DC: AEI-Brookings Joint Center for Regulatory Studies, 2000), page 93. See also page 31: "[A]t most, the AOL acquisition of Netscape may increase the rents that Microsoft has to pay to AOL" (to have AOL keep using IE).

illegal conduct.[14]

After the conclusion of the Microsoft trial, AOL/Netscape brought out Netscape 6, a long-awaited upgrade. The company denied it had delayed the launch in order not to undermine the Microsoft prosecution, but the timing was certainly fortuitous.

Like earlier versions of the AOL-owned Netscape browser, Netscape 6 steers users toward the AOL instant messaging chat program.[15] AOL/Netscape owns 90 percent of the instant messaging market,[16] and has worked assiduously to prevent users of competing instant messengers (e.g., Yahoo!'s) from communicating with AOL customers. AOL/Netscape has refused repeated requests from the rest of the instant messaging companies to allow interconnection.

Netscape 6 also steers visitors to the Netscape Web portal, the sixth-most-visited site on the entire Internet, far outranking Microsoft's competing portal. The Netscape portal, in turn, promotes e-commerce with various AOL/Netscape affiliates.[17]

There is nothing legally wrong with AOL/Netscape's conduct, either now or in 1994. It is doubtful that these efforts—even by the leading browser manufacturer and the leading Internet Service Provider—will establish a chokehold on the Internet.

Netscape did have a monopoly, as some economists define monopoly, from 1994 to 1996, and Netscape behaved like a monopolist, injuring companies such as Eudora in the process. Today, AOL/Netscape continues to act in a monopolist fashion in the instant messaging market. As the Netscape story shows, monopolies in the Digital Economy are quite vulnerable to competition, and if monopoly prices get too high (like Netscape's $49 charge for a piece of simple software), competitors can undercut the monopoly, as Microsoft did by offering Internet Explorer for free.

Were the Department of Justice consistent, Netscape and Microsoft both would have been prosecuted under the Sherman Act. Yet the failed monopolists

---

[14]This is not to say Fisher and Rubinfeld are stupid. The point is that no one can confidently forecast the long term of the Digital Economy. It is hubris to make such forecasts, and for a company to be punished on the basis of such forecasts is no more just than for a company to be punished based on the expert testimony as to how the Oracle at Delphi read some entrails.

[15]Paul Festa, "Short Take: AOL Updates Communicator," http://news.cnet.com/, October 25, 2000.

[16]Instant messaging allows people who are logged onto the Internet to communicate immediately by having a typed conversation in real time. This is faster than email, for which the delay between sending and receiving a message may be seconds or hours.

[17]Nick Wingfield, "Browser Wars, Version Two: Netscape's Back," *Wall Street Journal*, April 5, 2000.

from Netscape wax indignant about Microsoft's invasion of their monopoly territory, and they incited the Department of Justice to prosecute Microsoft for doing what they themselves had done and apparently planned to continue doing. It would be difficult to find a match for this level of hypocrisy.

NEW INDUSTRIAL POLICY

Netscape's Marc Andreeson had helped drive Netscape's market valuation sky-high when he claimed that Netscape, as middleware, would become the new computing platform, leaving Windows as merely a "poorly debugged set of device drivers."[18]

But at trial, the government's economic expert, Dr. Frederick Warren-Boulton, admitted Netscape's browser had never been a potential all-purpose platform: "One cannot easily write any application for Communicator.[19] One would find it very difficult, for example, to write a general ledger package or a word processor using these APIs. But an online banking application would be relatively straightforward to write."[20]

Even for simpler applications (*e.g.*, online banking), Netscape never even attempted to make its browser modular, which would have been of considerable assistance to software developers who wanted to write for a Netscape platform. Nevertheless, the Department of Justice insists Netscape would have had hope as a middleware platform if not for Microsoft.

A much more realistic picture of the situation would be that Microsoft pulled Netscape's market share down from 90 percent to 42 percent, benefitting consumers and countless dot.coms in the process. Now that AOL is switching to Netscape, Netscape and Microsoft are likely to trade market shares, staying in the 40 percent/60 percent range unless one of the companies, or a new competitor, introduces a superior browser.

Is this largely unintended outcome a great competitive situation, which emerged without the controlling assistance of the federal government? Not according to the DOJ and Judge Jackson. According to their theory, Microsoft *harmed* competition when it undercut Netscape's market share. Under the DOJ/Jackson theory, sufficient developers would start writing applications for

---

[18]John Heilemann, "The Truth, the Whole Truth and Nothing but the Truth," *Wired*, November 2000, page 275.

[19]The browser is still named Navigator but is now bundled with email and other applications as part of a suite called Communicator.

[20]Cross-examination of Dr. Frederick Warren-Boulton, *United States v. Microsoft*, December 1, 1999, page 67.

Netscape only if they believed Netscape would be the dominant platform.[21] This theory is the "applications barrier to entry" hypothesis discussed earlier with respect to the Windows OS. It still fails to explain why sufficient developers wrote applications for DOS, long before DOS appeared capable of overtaking CP/M as the dominant platform.

The DOJ's embrace of Netscape suggests antitrust can be used as a form of industrial policy, call it the New Industrial Policy,[22] in which federal employees attempt to steer the private assets of investors and companies in directions they, the federal employees, divine to be in the best interests of the country. Industrial policy of this sort was popular in Japan for awhile, as the Ministry of Industry and Trade (MITI) decided which companies should prosper and which should not, and it was often cited as a model for U.S. economic policy.[23] The collapse of the Japanese bubble in the mid-1990s discredited this industrial policy,[24] but it apparently still has adherents in the Department of Justice.

To believe in the DOJ New Industrial Policy, one would have to accept the following assumptions:

1. Despite its creator's own reservations, Netscape could have become a major applications platform.

2. The principal obstacle to Netscape becoming a major applications platform was an attachment by application developers to Windows.

3. Whereas the Windows monopoly was bad for consumers and the computing industry as a whole, a Netscape monopoly would be a good monopoly.

DOJ policy, then, is to punish any company that competes with the company DOJ has decided shows the most promise to develop a useful product sometime in the future. By introducing browser competition today, Microsoft reduced the possibility that, sometime in the future, another kind of competition

---

[21]David S. Evans and Richard L. Schmalensee, "The Economics of the Microsoft Antitrust Case: A Post-Trial Primer," *supra* note 10, page 76.

[22]See Claude E. Barfield and William A. Schambra, editors, *The Politics of Industrial Policy* (Washington, DC: American Enterprise Institute, 1986); Don Lavoie, *National Economic Planning: What is Left?* (Washington, DC: Cato Institute, 1985); and Richard B. McKenzie, *The American Job Machine* (New York, NY: Universe Books, 1988).

[23]Robert B. Reich, *Tales of a New America* (Washington, DC: Times Books, 1987), pages 70-77, 231.

[24]Jeffrey Bartholet, "Dimming the Sun," *Newsweek*, March 17, 1997, pages 38-39.

(operating system) might develop. If this reasoning seems counterintuitive to the reader, it is only because it is.

Interestingly, most of the Netscape managers who knew so much about middleware, but did so little to make it happen, are now gone. Netscape is owned by AOL, whose 25 million customers are generally reckoned to be the least-sophisticated group of Web users,[25] making them an unlikely group to put in charge of the future of browser and OS evolution.

AOL has already used Netscape to develop a calendar program for AOL, and AOL may well use Netscape as a platform to develop other types of software for AOL customers.[26] Regardless of what happens in the rest of the Internet, AOL's 25 million customers now provide a more-than-sufficient base for Netscape to get its chance to perform as middleware.

THE AOL DEAL

In Judge Jackson's Findings of Fact, no act was more pernicious than "the AOL coup"—the judge's term for Microsoft's temporary alliance with America Online.

With the Netscape/Microsoft browser war in progress, America Online decided to take advantage of the situation. AOL's proprietary browser was widely derided as slow and unreliable; AOL knew that as the Web continued to become more important, AOL's customers needed a better browser. In late 1995, AOL approached both Netscape and Microsoft to inquire about using their browsers in the next new version of AOL software. The Microsoft browser had an important technological advantage: Its modular design made it much easier for AOL to customize the browser and integrate it into the rest of the AOL software. Also, Microsoft was much more supportive with technical assistance.

Both Netscape and Microsoft owned property that could help recruit AOL customers. Netscape's Web portal was one of the most popular on the Internet, far ahead of Microsoft's, and could be used to encourage people to sign up for AOL. Microsoft's portal was not particularly attractive to AOL, but the Windows desktop was. Microsoft could place an AOL sign-up icon on every

---

[25]When AOL began giving its subscribers Internet access in the early 1990s, Internet veterans were incensed as AOL "newbies" flooded into use.net discussion groups, failing to obey established and elementary standards of courtesy and competence. WebTV users are even less sophisticated than AOL users, but their numbers are more than an order of magnitude smaller than AOL's subscriber base.

[26]Richard B. McKenzie, *Trust on Trial, supra* note 3, page 43.

new Windows desktop.[27] Microsoft agreed to let AOL onto the Windows desktop, while Netscape refused to allow AOL to manage the Netscape portal. So AOL chose to contract with Microsoft.[28]

To an ordinary person, it might seem that AOL's choice was a reasonable business decision, based on the fact that Microsoft offered better terms than Netscape. If there were an antitrust issue in the arrangement, suspicion would logically be cast on Netscape, which at the time of the bargaining (late 1995) had over 90 percent of the browser market. Yet Judge Jackson found that by coming to terms with AOL, Microsoft had attempted to "monopolize" a market in which another company held over 90 percent.

AOL bought Netscape in January 1998, thus gaining control of Netscape's Web portal and laying the basis for AOL to replace IE with Netscape. Judge Jackson's Findings of Fact, however, do not refer to this as "the AOL Counter-Coup."

SUPPLYING INTERNET EXPLORER FOR FREE

Another way in which Microsoft was said to have violated antitrust laws was by giving Internet Explorer away for free.[29] Despite what DOJ believed, the commercially realistic price of an Internet browser *is* zero, since browsers are so inexpensive to produce. That is why there are over three dozen browsers currently available for free. But let us suppose that browsers could today be sold for a profit—as they briefly were before Netscape's overpricing attracted competition. In the name of protecting consumers from monopoly price gouging, DOJ attempted to force a company to *stop* giving a product away. How do consumers benefit from having to pay Microsoft more money as a "remedy" for Microsoft's monopoly?

Similarly, much of the 1969-1982 government antitrust case against IBM was founded on charges that IBM set its prices too low, such as by giving education discounts. In fact, giving a product away for free is a good way for market entrants to challenge the dominant company. Thus, IBM gives away Lotus Notes almost for free. Yahoo! has challenged Internet auction king eBay

---

[27]As it turns out, AOL overestimated the power of the Windows desktop. Although exact figures are proprietary to AOL, the company acknowledges that only a small percentage of new customers come from desktop referrals.

[28]David S. Evans and Richard L. Schmalensee, "The Economics of the Microsoft Antitrust Case: A Post-Trial Primer," *supra* note 10, page 55.

[29]Jackson Findings of Fact, ¶ 140 (noting Microsoft spent $100 million annually to develop IE and $30 million to promote it).

by creating a free auction service.[30]

Giving away a product is no sure road to success, however, if the product is inferior. Microsoft has given its SQL database away for free, but has only a 4 percent market share, compared to 39 percent for Oracle.[31] Likewise, Microsoft has given away a free firewall program (to protect computers from Internet intruders), but it is not the market leader.

Microsoft has promised it will *never* charge for Internet Explorer. Should Microsoft break that promise, Internet portals such as Yahoo!, and Internet Service Providers such as Earthlink, can be expected to respond quickly with their own free browsers.[32]

The idea that a product that is free now, and will have to be free forever, can be the basis of a predatory pricing claim shows how perfectly malleable antitrust is. Netscape's business strategy of giving away its browser for free and then charging $49 after competitors left the market could have been the subject of a conventional antitrust lawsuit in 1995, yet it is Microsoft's much more consumer-friendly strategy of always-free that is the target of an antitrust suit.

Yale Law Professor John Lott recently questioned whether predatory pricing should still be part of antitrust theory.[33] His careful search and econometric analysis found that companies that attempt predatory pricing hardly ever recoup the profits they lose by setting prices so low. When the company, having eliminated a competitor, tries to raise prices to recapture the lost profits, new competitors often enter the market.

RECIPROCAL ADVERTISING AND PROMOTION

Many businesses enter into reciprocal promotional arrangements. If a retail store's advertisement in the Yellow Pages mentions the store is a "Certified Dealer for Wombat Products," then the Wombat company may give the retail store a discount on wholesale Wombat purchases. Similarly, discounts are offered if an OEM puts the Windows logo on a computer, the box, or the company's Web site. Intel offers a similar discount for companies that display the "Intel inside" logo.

---

[30]"How the Net Is Changing Competition," *Fortune*, March 15, 1999, page 168.

[31]"Microsoft's Future," *Business Week*, January 19, 1998, page 66.

[32]Chris E. Hall and Robert E. Hall, *National Policy on Microsoft: A Neutral Perspective, supra* note 1, pages 41-42.

[33]John R. Lott Jr., *Are Predatory Commitments Credible?* (Chicago, IL: University of Chicago Press, 1999).

Reciprocal Promotions
with Internet Service

Reciprocal promotional agreements frequently require that one company be favored over its competitors. For example, consider this hypothetical offering from a brewer: The Dinglehoffer Beer Company will offer an extra 20 percent discount to liquor stores that feature Dinglehoffer's name in type larger than the type used for any other beer company name in the store's Memorial Day advertising. This kind of arrangement is, in antitrust law, a weak form of "exclusive dealing." A strong form of exclusive dealing would be to forbid the liquor store from selling any beer other than Dinglehoffer. Some of Microsoft's reciprocal promotions were intermediate forms of exclusive dealing.

An Internet Service Provider (ISP) supplies the link between a consumer's computer and the rest of the Internet. There are many hundreds of ISPs in the United States. Windows comes with an Internet Connection Wizard that guides consumers, if they choose to run the Wizard, through the process of choosing an ISP and signing up for Internet access. Microsoft entered into reciprocal arrangements with a dozen ISPs to be featured in the Internet Connection Wizard. Microsoft waived many of the contract terms contained in those agreements in 1998, before the DOJ case had been filed, but the role they played prior to the waiver is an important issue in the antitrust suit.

For every customer the ISP signed up thanks to the Internet Connection Wizard referral, Microsoft would get a referral fee. Many Web surfers use the browsers they are given by their ISP. For the dozen featured ISPs, Microsoft required the ISP use the Microsoft Internet Explorer (IE) Web browser as the default browser *for those customers.*

The most controversial terms, however, applied to new ISP customers who did *not* come to the ISP via Microsoft's referral. ISPs could distribute non-Microsoft browsers (primarily, the Netscape browser) to up to 25 percent of those customers. ISPs were required to meet a target of 75 percent or more of their customers using IE. ISPs could not promote other browsers except in response to specific customer requests.

These ISP contracts may pose the greatest problem to Microsoft during its appeal. Most of the rest of Judge Jackson's findings against Microsoft involve violations of Section Two of the Sherman Act, and none of the underlying acts is a violation if the appeals court finds Microsoft is not a monopoly. But exclusive dealing is considered a "restraint of trade" under Section One of the Sherman Act, which applies to all companies, not just monopolies.

While Microsoft waived many of these contract terms in 1998, it still enforces the term that Netscape cannot be given preferred promotion over

Microsoft. That the others terms were voluntarily waived by Microsoft does not remove them as an antitrust issue, since the terms could someday be used in a future contract between Microsoft and ISPs.

In addition, Microsoft offered ISPs all over the country (not just the dozen ISPs featured in the Internet Connection Wizard) an Internet Explorer Access Kit. This kit allowed ISPs to customize Internet Explorer and attach the ISP's brand to Internet Explorer. So when the consumer ran the IE browser, he would see the ISP's logo and name. If an ISP made Internet Explorer its "preferred browser" (the browser ordinarily distributed to customers via disks, CD-ROM, or download), then the customization kit was free. The ISPs were allowed to distribute other browsers, so long as IE was the default choice. Netscape did not even offer ISPs a customization kit until June 1997, and the kit, when finally introduced, cost $1,995.[34]

James Rill, a former DOJ lawyer who now represents Microsoft's competitors, charges that Microsoft's reciprocal relations with ISPs amount to "keeping competitors off the field."[35] Actually, Microsoft's ISP customization kit *created* a new playing field that Netscape lethargically ignored.

Reciprocal Promotions with Web Sites

One of the new features of Windows 98 was the Channel Bar. The bar was really nothing more than a glorified "favorites list"—a listing of particular Web sites that could be accessed just by clicking on the site's name. While consumers could add or remove sites on the Channel Bar, an unmodified Channel Bar contained links to two dozen Web sites with reciprocal arrangements with Microsoft.

The "travel" slot on the Channel Bar went to Microsoft's own travel Web site, Expedia. This supposedly gave Expedia an unfair advantage over other travel Web sites, such as Travelocity. Almost all of the other channel slots, however, were given to independent Web sites, such as Walt Disney, Warner Brothers, and the (now-defunct) Pointcast news service.

Web sites that received initial placement on the IE Channel Bar could promote Netscape as much or as little as they wanted—but they had to agree not

---

[34]David S. Evans and Richard Schmalensee, "The Economics of the Microsoft Antitrust Case: A Post-Trial Primer," *supra* note 10, pages 55-56.

[35]James F. Rill, "Why Bill Gates is Wrong," *Wall Street Journal*, November 20, 1997.

to promote Netscape on the single page (the Web site home page) to which the IE Channel link would send surfers. Netscape cut a similar deal with ABC.com; Netscape would steer Web browsers to ABC, and ABC agreed not to promote Internet Explorer on its home page.

The IE Channel Bar's preferred Web sites also promised not to pay other browser companies in order to be promoted by those companies. This prevented a conflict of interest that might reduce the incentive for the Web site to encourage its customers to use Internet Explorer. There were, of course, millions of additional Web sites—and dozens of additional major Web sites in the categories covered by IE Channels—that remained available for Netscape to offer deals similar to the deal Microsoft cut with its Channel allies.

Channels failed. They simply did not add much traffic to the targeted Web sites. Indeed, the Windows desktop has been considerably less successful at steering consumers to specific Web sites than Microsoft had hoped or its competitors had feared.

Even if the Channel Bar promotion had been successful, it should not be labeled an anti-competitive act under antitrust law. Nor should the other reciprocal agreements between Microsoft and various Internet companies. Agreements of the type described above are ubiquitous on the Internet as hundreds of thousands of Web sites search for ways to attract traffic and add value to their sites. What distinguishes Microsoft from the rest of the pack is not the terms of the agreements, but Microsoft's size and prominence, which made it an easy target for regulators.

Such agreements are invariably win-win propositions for businesses and consumers alike. As Robert Bork wrote in *The Antitrust Paradox*:

> The truth appears to be that there has never been a case in which exclusive dealing or requirements contracts were shown to injure competition. A seller who wants exclusivity must give the buyer something for it. If he gives a lower price, the reason must be that the seller expects the arrangement to create efficiencies that justify the lower price.[36]

OEMs and Internet Explorer

When licensing Windows to original equipment manufacturers (OEMs), Microsoft insisted that Internet Explorer be included. This was true for

---

[36]Richard B. McKenzie, *Trust on Trial*, *supra* note 3, page 208.

Windows 95, for which IE 1.0 was a supplemental program, and for Windows 98, which integrated IE 4.0 into the operating system itself. Microsoft never charged extra for IE; it was simply a mandatory part of the Windows OEM package.

Notably, Microsoft never even sought contract terms from any OEM to forbid the OEM from also including Netscape. Microsoft simply insisted that IE be included on the desktop. OEMs were free to add other software, including from Netscape.[37] OEMs could, if they chose, set Netscape to be the default browser.

By contrast, Netscape *did* attempt to foreclose OEMs from shipping IE. Netscape offered to pay OEMs *not* to include IE on the desktop. Those offers were made at a time when Netscape's market share was at "monopoly" level, and the payment-to-exclude-IE offers were an obvious form of exclusive dealing. Yet in the Kafkaesque world of antitrust, the DOJ took no action against the dominant company that tried to exclude its smaller competitor. Instead, it was the maker of the upstart product who was sued for illegal "exclusion."

During the trial it was alleged that, during a 1994 meeting between Microsoft and Netscape, Microsoft urged Netscape to stay out of the Windows browser business and to concentrate on the Apple market instead. Employees from Microsoft and Netscape tell very different stories about the meeting, and some subsequent emails and memos from Netscape are not entirely consistent with Netscape's version. Judge Jackson's finding that the Netscape version of the story was the true story is unlikely to be overturned on appeal, since appellate courts are very deferential to a trial judge's evaluation of the credibility of conflicting witnesses. Whatever happened at that meeting, it is undisputed that Microsoft subsequently provided Netscape with access to the Windows APIs, so that Netscape could write a browser for Windows 95.

Because some OEMs thought one browser was enough and two would lead to more work for their customer support staffs, the fact that IE would be on every new Windows desktop made these OEMs decide not to include Netscape in their pre-installed software. Netscape, egging on the Department of Justice to file suit, claimed Netscape had been foreclosed from giving away its browser via OEM sales to consumers.

But a report by AOL's investment bankers, Goldman, Sachs, prepared for AOL's purchase of Netscape, stated Netscape was pre-installed on 22 percent

---

[37]Robert Levy, "Microsoft Redux: Anatomy of a Baseless Lawsuit," *Policy Analysis* No. 352 (Washington, DC: Cato Institute, 1999), page 7.

of computers.[38] In January 1999, Compaq (in exchange for a payment from Netscape) began installing Netscape on its new machines.[39] The apparent perjury of a star government witness was mostly ignored by the media.

Another OEM issue in the antitrust case concerned the initial screen consumers see the very first time they turn on their computers, called the startup screen. Microsoft insisted that OEMs not replace the Windows startup screen with a customized screen. OEMs could add as many icons as they wanted, but OEMs could not remove the icons Microsoft included.

As a matter of copyright law, Microsoft was plainly within its rights to insist that its software display not be altered. The trial court, however, found Microsoft's copyright irrelevant.

After the initial boot, changing the startup screen once and for all takes only a few mouse clicks. OEMs could always include icons (along with supporting paperwork) to tell a user to "Click here to start your Gateway experience." From there, the OEM could customize at will, steering the user into the OEM's preferred Internet Service Provider, or wherever else the OEM wanted the user to go.

If steering from the initial boot (rather than from the first screen after the initial boot) were really all that important, OEMs could have paid Microsoft to acquire such steering rights. Nothing prevented the OEMs and Microsoft from coming to mutually satisfactory terms.[40] The effect of Department of Justice intervention, however, was to give the OEMs some of Microsoft's property rights without the OEMs having to pay for them.

A society that believes people are capable of calling an 800 number to switch telephone companies might also assume reasonably that many of them are capable of following menu instructions to change the startup screen on their PCs. It is remarkable, in hindsight, that so much attention was devoted to so minor a detail that, if important to OEMs, could have been readily solved by negotiation, and, if important to consumers, could have been solved with a few keystrokes.

---

[38]David S. Evans and Richard L. Schmalensee, "The Economics of the Microsoft Antitrust Case: A Post-Trial Primer," *supra* note 10; Joseph Nocera, "The Big Blue Diaries," *Fortune*, July 5, 1999, page 134.

[39]Franklin M. Fisher and Daniel L. Rubinfeld, "*United States v. Microsoft*: An Economic Analysis," *supra* note 13, page 117, note 50.

[40]Ronald A. Cass, "Copyright, Licensing, and the 'First Screen,'" *Michigan Telecommunications and Technology Law Review* 5:35-71 (1998-1999).

TYING AND BUNDLING

Antitrust doctrine forbids "tying" or "bundling" two separate products together. In one classic case, IBM was prosecuted for requiring companies that bought IBM computers to also buy IBM punch cards to use in the computers.[41] The scope of what is forbidden is so enormous that it would be difficult for many businesses *not* to violate the law sometime.

Existing anti-tying/bundling rules could be used to prosecute hotels for providing mini-bars in their rooms (unfair competition against local liquor stores) and bars of soap by the sinks (unfair competition with the nearby drug store), or to prosecute laptop computer manufacturers for including modems in all their computers (thus harming laptop users who never use email or the Internet). If these examples seem absurd, recall that General Motors was once prosecuted for putting its own brand of radios into GM cars.

In short, the prohibition on tying, like the other prohibitions in antitrust law, creates a world in which everyone is technically guilty, and therefore antitrust prosecutors enjoy the luxury of being able to select targets at will. That this situation is dangerous to economic and civil liberties was recognized by the U.S. Supreme Court as far back as 1878, when it held in *United States v. Reese*, "It could certainly be dangerous if the legislature could set a net wide enough to trap all possible offenders, and leave it to the courts to step inside and say who could rightfully be detained, and who should be set at large."[42]

Many economists reject the whole doctrine of tying.[43] They argue the monopolist will be able to earn only whatever monopoly profits the actual monopoly provides. Tying the monopoly product to another product may rearrange the cash flow, but the tying cannot increase how much consumers are willing to pay, in the long run, to obtain the monopoly product.

The tying charges against Microsoft are ludicrous even by antitrust precedent.[44] The intent of tying is to keep the company from using monopoly

---

[41]If the computer/punch card tie was ever a real problem, it was eventually solved by technological advance. Punch cards were rendered obsolete by the development of electronic storage on disks. Gary S. Becker, "The Feds Should Let Microsoft Be Microsoft," *Business Week*, December 1, 1997, page 24.

[42]92 U.S. 214, 221 (1878).

[43]Richard A. Posner, *Antitrust Law: An Economic Perspective* (Chicago, IL: University of Chicago Press, 1976), pages 171-211; Dominick T. Armentano, *Antitrust and Monopoly: Anatomy of a Policy Failure* (Oakland, CA: Independent Institute, second edition, 1990), chapter 7.

[44]For a lengthier and excellent analysis of tying doctrine as applied to the Internet Explorer browser, see Robert A. Levy, "Microsoft and the Browser Wars: Fit to be Tied," *Policy Analysis* No. 296 (Washington DC: Cato Institute, February 19, 1998).

power in one market (*e.g.*, mainframe computers) to extract monopoly-level profits in a second, competitive market (*e.g.*, punch cards). In the Microsoft case, the "tied" product, Internet Explorer, *was given away for free*, making it difficult to imagine how profits from the browser market could offset the income deferred in the OS market.

The Economic Case for Integrating IE into Windows

Even if Netscape had not existed, it would have been eminently sensible for Microsoft to develop Internet Explorer and integrate it into Windows. In contrast to Windows 95, which was a radical redesign of the DOS/Windows 3.1 operating system, Windows 98 was only an incremental upgrade, with improved drivers, a slightly better interface, and technology-forcing support for the USB port. Those enhancements would be of interest to OEMs, especially those whose new computers were to have USBs, but the consumer who was satisfied with Windows 95 might not be persuaded to spend $89 for Windows 98.

The near-unanimous verdict of the computer magazines was: Consumers should upgrade because Windows 98 includes an integrated browser.[45] The point was not just to have browsing capability, but to have other parts of the operating system (*e.g.*, help files, directory lists) display in a format already familiar from Internet browsing. The computer magazines disagreed about whether the integrated browser made Windows 98 an upgrade everyone should get, or whether (even with IE) Windows 98 was optional. But it was very clear that *without* IE fully integrated, a much smaller set of consumers would have chosen to upgrade from Windows 95.

Internet Explorer cost about $100 million to develop. Most of the campaign to promote IE was inexpensive, since it traded resources that were free to Microsoft, such as Windows desktop space, for free advertising on popular Web sites and elsewhere. Microsoft incurred expenses in negotiating these agreements and also incurred expenses offering customer support for Internet Explorer. More expenses came from use of the Web servers through which people downloaded new versions of IE.

Microsoft made some money by using IE to steer people to its Web portal, where some of them engaged in e-commerce. But the simple economic fact is this: Without IE, Windows 98 sales to upgrading consumers would have been

---

[45]Especially positive reviews of IE include: Ed Bott, "Upgrade Windows and the Web," *PC Computing*, January 1998, page 117; Michael Miller *et al.*, "Memphis & IE 4.0," *PC Magazine*, September 1997, page 112; and Stephen H. Wildstrom, "Why I'm Rooting for Microsoft," *Business Week*, February 23, 1998, page 30.

vastly less. Increased consumer sales of Windows 98 more than earned back all of the money Microsoft had spent in developing and promoting IE. Indeed, Microsoft's efforts to make IE as ubiquitous as possible (even developing a version for Macintosh) helped pave the way for consumers to see IE as a comfortable, familiar, easy-to-use interface worth paying $89 to have extended throughout their operating systems. Spending many millions to help earn $3 billion in revenues from Windows 98 appears, from the outside at least, to be a reasonable business decision. A mere 3.5 percent increase in Windows 98 sales would have been enough for Microsoft to recoup its investment in IE.[46]

Since Microsoft also wants to encourage software programmers to write Windows applications, it had another good reason to include IE with every copy of Windows. Programmers could use the IE interface, which looks like a Web page, for many non-Web purposes, such as displaying help files. Users can browse back and forth between different help files just as they browse back and forth between Web pages. Also, users can click on a single hyper-linked word within a help document and jump to another document related to that word. Because of the ease of moving from file to file, IE displays help files far better than do the simple word processors Notepad and Wordpad, which were used to display help files in earlier versions of Windows.

From the software developer's point of view, Windows is advantageous because it performs much of the "drudge work" of programming. The programmer can write help files, connect them to the appropriate APIs, and leave it to Windows to take care of displaying the help file to consumers. If some Windows users have IE while others do not, the developer loses the standardization benefit that is the major point of Windows. The developer either has to write two help file routines (one for IE, another for Wordpad), or he has to put IE into his own program to make sure users will have IE. In either case, the developer is worse off than when he simply knows for sure that when he writes for Windows, he can use the IE tools.

By integrating IE, Microsoft enhanced the ability of Windows to attract and satisfy application developers. Microsoft has always worked very hard to support software developers. As discussed earlier, for example, the company gives a software development kit away for free. By contrast, IBM used to charge $600 for its OS/2 software development kit.[47]

---

[46]These figures are from Written Testimony of Paul Maritz, *United States v. Microsoft*, January 22, 1999, ¶ 293.

[47]Jerry Pournelle, "Jerry's Take On The Microsoft Decision: Wrong! Decision Neglects Industry History," *Byte*, November 8, 1999. The article notes various other errors IBM made that allowed OS/2 to be defeated by Windows.

While implementing an Internet Explorer strategy helped Microsoft make lots of money, Microsoft was *also* engaged in a jihad against Netscape. Almost every percentage point gained for IE would come at the expense of Netscape. And at least some Microsoft employees were worried (wrongly, it turns out) that Netscape could develop into an applications platform that would take market share away from Windows. Some of Microsoft's trouble at trial stemmed from employees' attempts to deny the jihad.

Thus, the DOJ case against Microsoft turns on the fact that *even though* Microsoft conducted a sensible business strategy, and *even though* this strategy benefitted consumers immensely, Microsoft is adjudged an antitrust violator because its actions were partly motivated by malice toward Netscape.

Integration Is an Important Strategy

The DOJ argued at length that Microsoft violated the law by putting Internet Explorer into Windows. Much of the DOJ's evidence consisted of attempts to prove that operating systems and Web browsers are in separate markets. Yet as Chris Hall and Robert Hall write, "Given the complete malleability of software, it seems pointless to debate the issue of whether one function of Windows 98 is separate or a part of the operating system. This is a debate at about the intellectual level of trying to decide if the Gulf of Mexico is part of the Atlantic Ocean."[48]

In 1993, when the World Wide Web was new, operating systems never included browsers. But as the Internet became the center of attention, every OS manufacturer began to include a browser in the OS. "The primary function of the OS, after all, has always been to enable applications to efficiently route data streams between the processor and peripherals. The Internet is the ultimate peripheral, and any OS that fails to incorporate a basic, standardized HTML engine today is inherently inefficient."[49]

Long before any consumer had even seen a copy of Windows 95, IBM was integrating a Web browser into its OS/2 operating system.[50] Sun integrates its

---

[48]Chris E. Hall and Robert E. Hall, *National Policy on Microsoft: A Neutral Perspective, supra* note 1, page 37.

[49]Rob Fixmer, "The Little Engine that Might," *Inter@ctive Week*, August 21, 2000, page 6.

[50]David S. Evans and Richard Schmalensee, "The Economics of the Microsoft Antitrust Case: A Post-Trial Primer," *supra* note 10; "Be Nice to Your Rivals: How the Government is Selling an Antitrust Case without Consumer Harm in *United States v. Microsoft*," in David S. Evans, Franklin M. Fisher, Daniel L. Rubinfeld, and Richard L. Schmalensee, *Did Microsoft Harm Consumers? Two Opposing Views, supra* note 13, page 51.

HotJava browser into its operating systems. A browser is part of the MacOS, and the BeOS touts its Opera browser as one of the OS's main virtues.

The fact is, as long as there have been operating systems, new versions of operating systems have been incorporating formerly separate products. Operating systems formerly did not include fonts. Now they do. Before Windows 3.0 introduced File Manager, operating systems did not have file management programs; one had to buy separate file management applications, such as Xtree.

The same is true for device drivers for CD-ROM support and built-in fax capability. If Microsoft is not permitted to harm competitors by integrating IE, what about all the other competitors who were harmed when Microsoft put Wordpad (as much word processing as the average home user will ever need), a calculator, a paint program, and dozens of computer management utilities (such as disk defragmentation and disk error scanning) into Windows?

Before Windows 95, file names could be no more than 11 characters long; users who wanted longer file names had to buy a special application program. Windows 95 integrated long file name support and thereby destroyed the separate market for long file name application programs. What makes Netscape worthy of protection by the Department of Justice while the creators of long file name applications are not?

The economics of software favors greater integration in several ways. Bundling different programs reduces sales and marketing expenses relative to revenues. Products can be more frequently updated by adding or replacing programs or upgrading some but not all of the programs in the bundle. Consumers rightly expect less hassle installing and using software, and a shorter learning curve when starting out, when programs are assembled into suites. All these reasons help explain why today's software suites are far less expensive than a single stand-alone word processing program was 15 years ago.[51]

HOW MICROSOFT BEAT NETSCAPE

Making OEMs include Internet Explorer and giving away IE for free were not the keys to Microsoft's (temporary) advantage over Netscape in the browser war. On the day Windows 95 was launched, every OEM computer included Internet Explorer 1.0. Still, Microsoft's share in the browser market was tiny compared to Netscape's. Having tried to charge retail consumers for IE in the August-December 1995 period—and having achieved a pitiful market

---

[51]Alan Reynolds, "Rear Windows," *National Review*, December 21, 1998, page 51.

share—Microsoft in December 1995 announced IE would be free forever. Version 2.0 was introduced and aggressively promoted. IE's market share remained pathetic. Version 1.0 had been panned by reviewers; version 2.0 was better, but by general consensus was inferior to Netscape 2.0.

With version 3.0, IE finally pulled even with Netscape in product quality, according to most reviewers.[52] Version 4.0 was clearly ahead of Netscape, most reviewers found, and Version 5.0 widened the gap still further.[53] Microsoft also offered better customer service. Internet Service Providers got a free software customization kit from Microsoft, but nothing from Netscape, until Netscape introduced a kit for $1,995. In short, Microsoft did not take the lead in the browser wars simply because it gave away a heavily promoted product. Microsoft closed the gap, and eventually took the lead, because it produced a *superior* product.

Many readers may be skeptical that a company devoted to high-volume/low-price can also be a leader in product innovation. It was often said during the Microsoft trial by Microsoft's critics that the company's products were mediocre and that it coopted or absorbed the inventors of new products to avoid having to compete.[54] In fact, Microsoft can take credit for an impressive number of technological firsts, including:[55]

- first programming language for a personal computer;

- first PC word processor to support a mouse;

- first word processor to use tables;

- first bundling of office productivity applications, at a price far below the cost of individual items;

- first retail mouse;

- first multimedia encyclopedia; and

---

[52]Stan J. Liebowitz and Stephen E. Margolis, *Winners, Losers & Microsoft* (Oakland, CA: Independent Institute, 1999), pages 219-222.

[53]Stan Liebowitz, "Bill Gates Secret? Better Products," *Wall Street Journal*, October 20, 1998, page A22.

[54]Richard B. McKenzie, *Trust on Trial, supra* note 3, page 130.

[55]*Ibid.*, pages 131-132, 137-138.

■   first spreadsheet program with pivot tables.

It should not be implausible, then, that Microsoft was able to win market share for IE by continuously improving the software until it was a more useful and attractive product to most consumers than other browsers.

Also contributing to IE's success was that since 1997, Microsoft allowed other companies to integrate IE into their programs. For example, Intuit, the manufacturer of Quicken (the leading home and business financial program), wanted Quicken users to be able to conduct Internet business (*e.g.*, visit Quicken's Web site, read Quicken-supplied stock analysis, browse to other financial news stories, or conduct online banking) without having to leave the Quicken program. Intuit had three choices: (1) pay Netscape or another browser company for the right to sell Netscape along with Quicken; but even then, the Netscape browser would run as a separate program and not as part of Quicken; (2) design its own, proprietary Web browser; or (3) integrate Internet Explorer into Quicken for free.

No surprise that Intuit chose the third option. Today, when the Quicken user browses the Web, he may not even know he is using the Microsoft browser. Netscape eventually started allowing software companies to integrate its browser into their programs, but as with so much else, Netscape's delay gave Microsoft a head start of several years (in Internet Time) and a considerable competitive advantage.[56]

A company named PowerBasic Inc., which was putting its Web site on a CD so customers could access information without having to go online, wanted to include a browser on the CD in case a customer did not already have a browser. Its CEO explained why he chose IE over Netscape:

> Being Netscape users, we first contacted Netscape by email to inquire about licensing. After no reply for a week, we tried calling them and constantly couldn't get anyone to help us. We were constantly told to send email. . . . Microsoft was ready and waiting for us with a license agreement and an easy download of IE 4.0 for our CD-ROM. All at no cost.[57]

Netscape has generally received better press than Microsoft, but it isn't clear its reputation as an innovator is deserved. A Web site developer dismisses all

---

[56]Rafe Needleman, "Microsoft's Smartest Move Ever," htttp://cnetnews.com, January 19, 1998.

[57]Dave Navarro, "Letters to the Editor," *Inter@ctive Week*, December 8, 1999, page 100.

the hype about Netscape as the epitome of a Digital Economy business:

> [O]ne of Netscape's strategies was to leverage Internet standards. However, the reality is that with its browser Netscape thumbed its nose at Internet standards, particularly when it dominated the market. Even today, its browser generally is seen as less compliant with standards than is Microsoft Explorer.
>
> Another alleged Netscape strategy was to "eat your own dog food," which means using your own products. The reality is quite different. For example, Netscape released a production version of Enterprise 3.0 and kept its own Web site on Enterprise 2.0 for several months afterward.
>
> In 1996, a key component of Netscape's Web server was something they called LiveWire, which provided scripting and database connectivity. I adopted it for my Web site in the second half of 1996. However, after several months of trying to get it to work reliably, we had to abandon it, moving to Java servlets instead.
>
> Meanwhile, as of late 1997 (when I stopped following it), Netscape's Web site still had not adopted LiveWire. They let other users suffer with the bugs and problems in LiveWire, while they ran their own site using the older technology of CGI/Perl. That means they spent at least 1-1/2 years in real time . . . NOT eating their own dog food. In contrast, Microsoft used their competing Active Server Page technology immediately on their sites.
>
> [M]y epitaph for Netscape is that it is a company that told the press and its shareholders that it was aiming to play in the Super Bowl, but disdained to practice blocking and tackling.[58]

Browser Choice
Is Alive and Well

When the antitrust case began, 10 years ago in Internet Time, the Department of Justice unsuccessfully asked the court for an order requiring Microsoft to distribute the Netscape browser pending litigation. "This would prevent the browser market from 'tipping' in favor of Microsoft during an extended court battle, officials

---

[58]Arnold Kling, review of Michael A. Cusumano and David B. Yoffie, *Competing on Internet Time: Lessons From Netscape & Its Battle with Microsoft*, http://www.amazon.com.

said."[59] Netscape is alive and well, and—under new management—poised to regain leadership in browser share in 2001, even without the DOJ's help. Even when Microsoft was ahead in the browser war, the market remained extremely competitive; that is why Microsoft brought out Internet Explorer 5.0 so rapidly—an innovation not to be expected from a monopolist.

Should Netscape disappear tomorrow, Internet Explorer would have no monopoly. There are 35 other browsers available for Windows.[60] Almost all of them are free.

According to U.S. Supreme Court Justice Sandra Day O'Connor, no tying case can be brought "if entry barriers in the tied-product market are low."[61] In the browser market, entry costs are so low that dozens of companies currently give the product away for free.

Justice O'Connor also writes that: "For products to be treated as distinct, the tied product must, at a minimum, be one that some consumers might wish to purchase separately without also purchasing the tying product."[62] In the Microsoft case, there is no consumer who would wish to purchase Internet Explorer for Windows without also purchasing the Windows operating system.

THE *LORAIN JOURNAL* CASE

Shortly after Netscape hired Robert Bork as its public advocate, Bork began steering public attention to a heretofore-obscure antitrust case called *Lorain Journal v. U.S.*[63] Here, wrote Bork, was the direct precedent for the Microsoft prosecution.[64]

In Lorain, Ohio, in the 1940s, the *Lorain Journal* was the only newspaper in town, and there was no radio station. When a radio station opened, the newspaper promptly informed its advertisers that if they advertised on the radio station, they would not be allowed to purchase print advertising from the *Lorain Journal*. In 1951, the U.S. Supreme Court ruled that this form of exclusive

---

[59]"U.S. Sues Microsoft on Antitrust Grounds," *Wall Street Journal*, May 19, 1998, page A3.

[60]www.browserwatch.com.

[61]*Jefferson Parish Hospital District No. 2 v. Hyde*, 466 U.S. 2, 33 (1984) (O'Connor, J., concurring).

[62]*Ibid.*, at page 39.

[63]*Lorain Journal v. United States*, 342 U.S. 143 (1951).

[64]Robert Bork, *The Case Against Microsoft*, http://www.procompetition.org/research/bork.html (1998).

dealing violated the Sherman Act.

That advocates of the anti-Microsoft case think their best precedent is a small 1940s town with only two forms of media, and that this precedent is useful in today's hypermedia world of the Internet, demonstrates the legal absurdity of the anti-Microsoft case and the obsolescence of antitrust.

Microsoft did not do what the *Lorain Journal* did: forbid customers from dealing with a competitor. OEMs that bought from Microsoft were free to install Netscape; Web sites and ISPs that received special promotion from Microsoft had to give Internet Explorer preferential promotion, but those companies could still distribute Netscape. And however much Microsoft's integration of a free version of IE into Windows may have been motivated by animus against Netscape, the integration provided obvious benefits to many consumers, whereas there was no consumer benefit from the *Lorain Journal's* attempted ban on the purchase of advertising on the local radio station.

The Lorain, Ohio of the 1940s is long gone. One Web media directory reports the town is now reached by 10 newspapers (including the *Lorain Morning Journal*) and four local television stations.[65] Add to this scores of cable television channels and the Internet—with 49 Web sites devoted mainly to Lorain content.[66] There are no towns left in America where the only way to communicate with the public is through a single newspaper or radio station.

The *Lorain* world disappeared with the arrival of Internet Time, making legal precedents from that era inapplicable to the Microsoft case or cases like it that are likely to emerge. No amount of control over the startup screen of personal computers can stop computer users from finding information online about competing producers of computers and software. And the marketplace for information about computers and software doesn't begin and end on the computer. America Online, for example, advertised on television, on the radio, in print, on billboards, and through direct mail; many other dot.coms seeking to build brand recognition do the same thing.

In a Brookings Institution/American Enterprise Institute book that contains chapters written by the expert economists on both sides of the Microsoft case, government economist Franklin Fisher makes a startling admission. Faced with evidence that, despite Microsoft's reciprocal arrangements with ISPs, Web sites, and OEMs, Netscape was very widely distributed, he claims it is still an antitrust problem "if Navigator was merely widely distributed or even widely installed

---

[65]www.newsdirectory.com.

[66]www.dmoz.org.

and not used."[67] For Netscape to become the middleware platform, it has to become "very widely *used* relative to IE."

In other words, if users have *both* IE and Navigator on their computer, and they choose to use IE, we still have an antitrust problem. It would be difficult to find a clearer admission that the mission of the Antitrust Division is to invent sophistries to protect inferior products.

BRIEFLY STATED . . .

For three years, Netscape's Navigator had a monopoly in the Web browser market. It lost that monopoly when Microsoft introduced Internet Explorer and gradually improved its quality and, in 1997, started encouraging the producers of other products to integrate IE into their programs and giving IE away to retail customers for free. With the pending switch of 25 million AOL members from IE to Netscape Navigator thanks to America Online's acquisition of Netscape, Navigator is likely to once again be the market leader.

It is puzzling that the DOJ would choose to overlook Netscape's monopolist past and anti-consumer practices (past and present) and target instead the company that broke up a monopolized market and gives away a superior product. The business practices used by Microsoft to promote IE were not exclusionary, and invariably worked to the benefit of consumers.

Why, then, the DOJ jihad against Microsoft? The possible explanation raised in this chapter is that Microsoft was a victim of industrial policy gone awry. Government officials, acting well beyond the limits of their competence or legal duties, tried to "pick a winner": a company whose leaders claimed its product, a Web browser, had the potential of becoming an applications platform that could eventually help another company compete successfully with Microsoft Windows in the operating system market.

The plan was doomed from the start. Even Netscape admits Navigator wasn't up to the task. Microsoft's decision to launch and aggressively market its own Web browser—a browser that quickly turned out to be superior to the regulators' Chosen One—ruined the plan and embarrassed its authors.

---

[67]Franklin M. Fisher and Daniel L. Rubinfeld, "Misconceptions, Misdirection, and Mistakes," in David S. Evans, Franklin M. Fisher, Daniel L. Rubinfeld, and Richard L. Schmalensee, *Did Microsoft Harm Consumers? Two Opposing Views, supra* note 13, page 93.

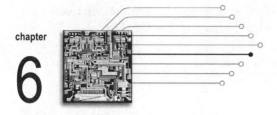

6

Crime and Punishment

Missing from the Microsoft case was real proof of actual harm to consumers today or at any time in the past. The phenomenon of antitrust violations being victimless crimes didn't start with the Microsoft case, but it has received a boost from it.

In 1999, the Federal Trade Commission brought an antitrust case against Intel, even though the FTC's own expert, Harvard professor F.M. Scherer, acknowledged there was no evidence Intel had harmed consumers.[1] After a company sued Intel in a patent dispute, Intel stopped giving it technical secrets about upcoming product designs. That a business ought to be able to stop voluntary cooperation with another company that sues it would appear to be common sense. Indeed, the FTC conceded Intel's behavior would be rational and appropriate for a normal business. But in the world of antitrust, companies with the scarlet "M-for-monopoly" are forbidden to do ordinary things.

---

[1]"Slippery Slope," *The Economist*, March 6, 1999, page 58.

NO CONSUMER HARM

On the witness stand, the government's chief economist in the Microsoft case, Franklin Fisher, acknowledged there had been no consumer harm:

Q. At the present time, have—in your analysis—consumers been hurt by Microsoft's conduct?

A. That's very hard to know . . . on balance, I would think that the answer was no, up to this point. The reason for that is that Microsoft has used its power to protect its operating systems monopoly from a threat that might not have materialized by this time anyway. And, in doing that, it has given away a lot of things.[2]

In a case that did not include testimony from a single consumer who alleged she had been harmed by Microsoft, U.S. District Judge Thomas Penfield Jackson found that by giving away a superior product for free, Microsoft "caused . . . serious and far-reaching consumer harm."[3] That harm was not of the sort usually attributed to monopolies, such as high prices or restricted output. By integrating IE into Windows 98, Judge Jackson found, Microsoft had harmed business customers who did not want hard disk space taken up by IE, or who did not want their employees to have access to the Internet. IE's inclusion in Windows, he found, made Windows run slower and raised the risk of bugs or viruses.[4]

One supposes Judge Jackson will next find that General Motors "harmed" consumers by pre-installing car radios: Dashboard space was taken up; consumers who did not want radios were burdened with extra buttons whose confusing effect might cause an accident; thieves might be attracted to the car, and automobile owners would therefore have to roll up their windows and lock their car doors to prevent a thief's entry; an automobile owner who liked to drive in silence would not be able to stop a passenger from surfing the airwaves.

In both cases, the harms are tangible, but do they rise to the level of being a matter of concern for the U.S. Department of Justice or, as may happen with the Microsoft case, the U.S. Supreme Court? It hardly seems reasonable to get the DOJ involved whenever a company's employees surreptitiously surf the

---

[2]Testimony of Franklin Fisher, *United States v. Microsoft*, January 12, 1999 (a.m. session).

[3]Jackson Findings of Fact, ¶ 409.

[4]*Ibid.*, ¶ 173, 410.

Internet. And is 17 cents' worth of hard disk space[5] on certain business computers really a matter of national concern?

> *A mountain in labour shouted so loud that everyone, summoned by the noise, ran up expecting that she would be delivered of a city bigger than Paris; she brought forth a mouse.*[6]

Judge Jackson also found a "dangerous probability" Microsoft would obtain "monopoly power" in the browser market.[7] Yet there is no evidence that Microsoft's "power" in any market has ever really harmed consumers. The "dangerous probability" rule in antitrust resembles the now-discredited "dangerous tendency" test used to justify censorship in the early twentieth century. Both tests serve mainly to punish politically unpopular defendants, even when the government cannot prove the defendant harmed anyone.

INNOVATION

Antitrust law has long had a difficult time coping with companies that innovate too much. A 1949 antitrust case against AT&T complained at length about the company's numerous innovations.[8] In the 1960s, in the famous *United Shoe* case, the court acknowledged the manufacturer of shoe-making machines had won its high market share through technological innovation and low-cost pricing. But those practices were held to have excluded competitors. The company was broken up, thereby destroying the domestic shoe manufacturing industry in the U.S.[9] The government investigated and prosecuted IBM, arguably the most innovative firm in the U.S. during the 1960s and 1970s, for

---

[5]Figure based on contemporary computer prices and the amount of space used by the browser in the new Windows Millennium Edition. Richard B. McKenzie, *Trust on Trial: How the Microsoft Case is Reframing the Rules of Competition* (Cambridge, MA: Perseus Books, 2000), page 61. Several years ago, when hard disk prices were higher, and when Internet Explorer 4.0 took up more disk space than would Internet Explorer 5.0, the harm might have amounted to a few dollars per computer.

[6]Jean de la Fontaine, "La Montagne qui Accouche" ("The Mountain in Labor"), in *Fables*, Volume V (1668).

[7]Conclusions of Law, *U.S. v. Microsoft*, April 3, 2000, page 22.

[8]Complaint, *United States v. Western Electric Co.*, No. 17-49 (D.N.J. January 14, 1949), at 14, discussed in Peter W. Huber, Michael K. Kellogg, and John Thorne, *Federal Telecommunications Law* (Laithersburg, NY: Aspen Publishing, 1999), page 355.

[9]*United States v. United Shoe Machinery Corp.*, 391 U.S. 244 (1968); *United States v. United Shoe Machinery Corp.*, 110 F. Supp. 295 (1953).

13 years, but never managed to create a coherent theory of the case.[10]

In the 1999-2000 fiscal year, Microsoft spent $3.8 billion on basic research.[11] Microsoft spent millions of dollars improving Internet Explorer after buying the rights to the original product from a small company. In his Findings of Fact, Judge Jackson complained about Microsoft's innovative conduct; even though Microsoft could have simply collected money from its OS "monopoly" for several years, with no innovation at all, the company spent too much money to build a better Web browser and then gave it away for free. Such innovation upset the plans and predictions of the court's cloistered experts by depriving Netscape of its 90 percent market share, thus ruining the Netscape-as-middleware scenario, which was supposed to undermine the Windows applications barrier to entry, which would perhaps have led to some other company directly challenging Microsoft's OS monopoly. While the court was busy creating these findings about how Microsoft's innovation might theoretically harm competition in the future, Linux started providing Microsoft with direct competition in the present, and the desktop computing market was rapidly being eclipsed by PDAs, net appliances, and Web-enabled cell phones.

Harvard Professor Larry Lessig, who Judge Jackson had tried to appoint as a hearing officer in the lawsuit over the 1995 Consent Decree, an appointment Microsoft prevented by appealing to the D.C. Court of Appeals, acknowledges that Microsoft is innovative, but he claims Microsoft illegally crushes innovation that threatens the company.[12] Like the "95 percent market share" claim, this claim was repeated uncritically in the media, but there is very little to support it. After trolling through Silicon Valley and the rest of the country for months, after a long-term and highly visible publicity campaign against Microsoft, DOJ was unable to produce a single witness, or cite a single fact, showing Microsoft had prevented some kind of innovation.

The closest DOJ came was showing that Microsoft convinced Intel not to proceed with Native Signal Processing, but this had the pro-competitive effect of allowing other chip manufacturers to run Windows, thus helping pave the way for massive cuts in the price of computer chips in recent years.

---

[10]James V. DeLong, "Don't Repeat IBM Debacle," *Wall Street Journal*, March 3, 1998.

[11]Dori Jones Yang, "The Empire Strikes Out," *U.S. News & World Report*, November 15, 1999, page 50.

[12]Lawrence Lessig, "A Letter to Bill," *The Industry Standard*, June 17, 2000, page 51.

REMEDIES

The formless nature of antitrust is well-illustrated by the shifting nature of the government's demands and the disconnect between the evidence at trial and the remedy awarded by the judge.

During the Microsoft trial, the government introduced evidence about how Microsoft competed against Netscape and bargained with computer manufacturers who wanted to pre-install Windows. At the end of the trial, Judge Jackson found several ways in which Microsoft had used its monopoly power, each related to promoting Internet Explorer:

1. By entering into agreements with computer manufacturers, Internet companies, and software companies for them to promote IE rather than Netscape;

2. By attempting to divide the browser market with Netscape (the 1994 meeting at which Microsoft allegedly urged Netscape to concentrate on the Apple market); and

3. By "tying" the sale of Internet Explorer to Windows.[13]

If one agrees with the government that its various examples of hard competition and bargaining constituted illegal use of monopoly power, then one might expect the government to seek remedies related to those "abuses." And indeed, some remedies did relate to the evidence at trial. For example, Judge Jackson ordered Microsoft to sell Windows at a fixed price (no discounts) to its 20 largest computer manufacturer customers. The consumer benefit of a prohibition against discounting is difficult to discern, but at least this remedy has something to do with the trial evidence.

But the DOJ also sought, and Judge Jackson awarded, a remedy that had nothing to do with the trial evidence: breaking Microsoft into two companies—one with Windows, the other with everything else—and forbidding the two new companies from cooperating in the future.

It is as if a supermarket were sued because people kept slipping on banana peels inside the store—and the judge ordered the supermarket to hire security guards for the parking lot. In normal business law, the remedy has something to do with the complaint: If the evidence shows a contract was breached, the contract-breaker must obey the contract and/or pay for the damages caused by

---

[13]Jackson Findings of Fact.

the breach. If a company committed libel or slander or some other tort, the company must undo the harm it caused (such as by corrective advertising) and pay damages to the victim. But in antitrust, there is no necessary connection between the "remedy" and the preceding complaint and evidence.

One attempt to link the punishment meted out by Judge Jackson to the alleged crime is to claim, as the DOJ does, that it is impossible to enforce conduct remedies against Microsoft. As proof, the DOJ points to its 1995 Consent Decree with Microsoft, which DOJ says should have prevented Microsoft from integrating IE into Windows. But the Decree specifically allowed Microsoft to integrate new features into Windows. The D.C. Court of Appeals, examining the terms of the Consent Decree, found Microsoft's conduct entirely lawful. Thus, the only misbehavior revealed was on the part of DOJ and its aggressive misinterpretation of the Consent Decree's language.

In the remedy phase of the trial (for which the judge refused to hear any evidence), a business association hostile to Microsoft filed an *amicus* brief, which Judge Jackson praised as very helpful.[14] The brief recited a litany of ways in which Microsoft had obeyed the terms of the 1995 Consent Decree, but while doing so did something the business group didn't like. For example, the Decree forbade Microsoft to offer particular contractual terms to one type of customer; Microsoft obeyed the Decree, but offered the contractual terms to other types of customers, as allowed by the Decree.

The *amicus* brief, which brims with hatred for Microsoft, nevertheless insists that the breakup would be wonderful for Microsoft employees. For example, creative software engineers will be liberated from bureaucracy when they work for a smaller company. The differences between bureaucratic oppression in a 35,000-person firm and a 17,500-person firm are not specified.

The Department of Justice called its proposal to split Microsoft in half a "reorganization." A similar flair for euphemism was displayed by Attorney General Janet Reno when she referred to tanks used during the ill-fated assault on the Branch Davidian group home in Waco, Texas as "a very good rent-a-car."[15] Perhaps King Solomon could have gotten the mothers to agree to chop the baby in half if he had said he was proposing only a "reorganization."[16]

---

[14]*Brief on Remedy of Amici Curiae Computer and Communications Industry Association and Software and Information Industry Association*, Civil Action No. 98-1233 (TPJ)(D.D.C.).

[15]United States House of Representatives, Subcommittee on Crime of the Committee on Judiciary and the Subcommittee on National Security, International Affairs, and Criminal Justice, Joint Hearings on *Activities of Federal Law Enforcement Agencies Toward the Branch Davidians*, 104th Congress, 1st Session, July 19-August 1, 1995 (Washington, DC: Government Printing Office, 1996), part 3, page 366.

[16] Later, the DOJ adopted Microsoft's preferred term, "divestiture."

The breakup is radical in the sense that it has nothing to do with Microsoft's supposed antitrust violations. The breakup is unprecedented in that there has never been an involuntary court-ordered breakup of *any* company under the Sherman Act. Previous involuntary separations, such as in the *Standard Oil* and *American Tobacco* cases, involved mostly undoing earlier mergers and acquisitions, rather than dividing a company that had expanded only through internal growth, not by merger.

One needn't go far to find a motive for choosing such a draconian remedy. When the DOJ and Judge Jackson misread the 1995 Consent Decree, Microsoft humiliated them publicly by winning in the District of Columbia Court of Appeals. When Judge Jackson ordered Microsoft to start producing Windows in a particular way, Microsoft did so, complying literally with the Judge's order, while announcing that the Jackson version of Windows was "broken" and would not work. A furious DOJ and judge complained that Microsoft's literal interpretation of their language had misconstrued what they had meant (and what they would have said, if they had known what they were talking about). Like everything else Judge Jackson ordered against Microsoft in the Consent Decree litigation, the Jackson software production order was voided by the Court of Appeals.[17] Ordering the Microsoft breakup, Judge Jackson cited Microsoft's legally vindicated insistence on its interpretation of the Consent Decree as proof that "Microsoft has proved itself untrustworthy in the past."[18]

At trial, Microsoft contested every government claim tenaciously, rather than admitting it was a "monopoly," as most of the press urged. After trial, Bill Gates had the temerity to tell his employees, "Microsoft is very clear that it has done absolutely nothing wrong."[19] Judge Jackson complained that Microsoft was still "convinced of its own innocence." The *New York Times'* Thomas Friedman observed, "if you read carefully Judge Thomas Penfield Jackson's ruling to split up Microsoft, you'll see this was . . . a case about attitude . . . an indictment of the attitude of the high-tech community in general toward government. . . . that is the real point of Judge Jackson's ruling: . . . Microsoft is a threat because it is big and deaf to some of the bedrock values of the American system."[20]

---

[17]*United States v. Microsoft*, 980 F. Supp 537 (D.D.C. 1997), *rev'd* (D.C. Cir. 1998).

[18]Jonathan Weber, "Just Right on Antitrust," *The Industry Standard*, October 2, 2000, page 11.

[19]Steve Lohr and Joel Brinkley, "Microsoft Management Tells Workers There Will Be No Breakup," *New York Times*, April 26, 2000, page C9, quoted as proof of the need for a breakup in SIIA brief, *supra* note 14, page 24.

[20]Thomas L. Friedman, "The Young and the Clueless," *New York Times*, June 9, 2000.

OFFICE AS THE WINDOWS-KILLER?

How exactly is the breakup supposed to help consumers? The DOJ forecasts that once the Office company is separated from the Windows company, it will develop an Office suite for Linux.[21] This in turn would help Linux develop into a genuine competitor to Windows.

The idea that the absence of an Office version for Linux is a significant barrier to Linux's becoming a major operating system for home and small office personal computers is absurd. Microsoft makes a version of Office for the Apple MacOS—an operating system with a 15 percent market share for new computers. The world's number one personal finance program, Intuit's Quicken, also has a MacOS version. Yet Apple is not, according to the DOJ, a viable competitor to Windows. Why would Office give Linux a greater boost?

There are plenty of other office productivity applications available for Linux. The best-known of these is Corel's WordPerfect Office 2000, which contains the WordPerfect word processor, Paradox database program, Corel Presentations, and the Quattro Pro spreadsheet program. WordPerfect imports and exports Microsoft Word files so well that the American Bar Association has certified that lawyers may use WordPerfect to edit Word documents with no risk of introducing errors or formatting changes.[22]

Another office productivity suite written for Linux is StarOffice, which Sun Microsystems gives away with its versions of Linux. StarOffice easily imports from and exports to MS Word. Transitioning employees from Microsoft Office for Windows to StarOffice for Linux is only a "trivial expense," one company explains, because StarOffice so closely mimics the Microsoft Office interface.[23]

The DOJ breakup remedy is premised on the idea that Microsoft applications developers are not producing Office for Linux and other applications because they are being suppressed by Windows people who want to maintain the "applications barrier to entry" for Windows. The DOJ subpoenaed millions of pages of Microsoft's internal documents and email looking for incriminating phrases that might support this theory. Not a single sentence in any Microsoft paper or email was found.

The fact is that Microsoft, whether in its current form or chopped in half, has good business reasons for not producing an Office version for Linux. First, the entire program would have to be re-written from the ground up. Although Office

---

[21]Plaintiffs' Memorandum in Support of Proposed Final Judgment, *United States v. Microsoft*, April 28, 2000.

[22]www.abanet.org.

[23]"Linux Vendors Try to Practice What They Preach," *Inter@ctive Week*, May 29, 2000, page 99.

for Macintosh looks a lot like Office for Windows from the user's perspective, the code for the programs is entirely different, and Windows code cannot be exported to MacOS code. Creating an Office for Linux would mean creating an entirely new programming group, just as there is currently a separate group at Microsoft which programs Office for Macintosh. Would Linux's market share (nearly non-existent, according to the DOJ) justify such a massive undertaking? If split from the OS company, couldn't the "Applications Company" find a more profitable use of its talent and money?

While Office for Windows is very profitable for Microsoft, it would be difficult to predict any profit at all from entering the Linux market against competitors, such as Sun, that give their products away for free. As for the part of the market willing to pay for a suite, the leading Linux suite, WordPerfect Office 2000 for Linux, is available for $109, versus $249 for Microsoft Office for Windows.[24] So Microsoft would get all the headaches of having to develop entirely new Office code for a new operating system, while reaping the reward of much less profitable sales in a significantly smaller market.

Finally, antitrust law itself provides a disincentive to Microsoft writing an Office for Linux. Competition for Linux office suites could develop precisely as it did in the pre-Windows DOS arena. WordPerfect started out with a very large early lead, but WordPerfect's owners failed to keep up with evolutions in the operating system. As a result, WordPerfect consumers began noticing they had more difficult installations, more problems interfacing with the operating system, and more frequent crashes than did users of Microsoft Office. Suppose Microsoft Office displaced WordPerfect Office 2000 as the top Linux office suite. Would Microsoft's competitors once again run to the Antitrust Division and demand that the Division "do something" about Microsoft winning again? Why should Microsoft take the chance?

OFFICE AS MIDDLEWARE

We've observed before that the Department of Justice displayed tremendous intellectual flexibility throughout the Microsoft case. Faced with the counter-argument that Office could never be the savior for Linux, the DOJ responded it had never actually meant that an Office for Linux would be the key to Linux becoming much more popular and thereby challenging the Windows "monopoly." What the DOJ had really meant all along was that Office would develop into a kind of cross-platform middleware. There would be an Office for

---

[24]Charles Babcock, "Would Baby Bill Port to Linux?" *Inter@ctive Week*, May 8, 2000, page 14.

Windows, for Mac, and for Linux. Developers would start writing applications that would call on the Office APIs. As developers wrote fewer programs for Windows, and more for Office middleware, the Windows "applications barrier to entry" would be weakened.

This theory has several problems. There are over 12,000 programs for Apple computers, but these are supposedly not enough to negate the might of the Windows applications barrier to entry. What are the prospects that there would ever be 12,000 programs written for Office? Even if every single one of these Office programs for Linux or MacOS meant one less Windows program, Windows (with 70,000 programs already) would still have an overwhelming lead.

Moreover, there is no good reason to believe Office middleware would ever attract 1,200 programs, much less 12,000. Office is an adequate platform for developers who want to add sophistication to the Office applications; for example, a developer can write a program that works with Excel's spreadsheets and customizes Excel for use in an accounting firm. But these program customizations and extensions are a far cry from independent applications. Nobody would (for example) write a game or digital photography program that used Office APIs. Office would have to be massively rewritten and radically redesigned in order to serve as genuine middleware.

Why would an economically sensible company try to turn a popular application into middleware—especially when the program is already criticized as overly large "bloatware" with too many features?[25] One might ask why Intuit has not tried to turn Quicken (which is far more prevalent on home computers than is Microsoft Office) into middleware.

Even assuming that it might be economically sensible for a company that owned nothing but Microsoft Office to try to reinvent the product as middleware, it would not be sensible for the Microsoft Applications Company to do so. The applications company would own not just Office, but scores of other Windows products. To develop Office as middleware would be to undermine all those other Windows applications.

We know from the DOJ's complaints about the Microsoft/Netscape fight that when Microsoft brought Netscape's market share down from 90 percent to between 40 and 60 percent, it ruined Netscape's potential to develop into important middleware. Accordingly, it would seem that in order for Office to develop into important middleware, it is going to have to achieve a 90 percent or more market share on every operating system and create an expectation that this market share will endure over the long term.

---

[25]"Give Us a Simpler 'Office,'" *Business Week Online*, July 5, 1999.

Notwithstanding the unfriendly relationship between Microsoft and the DOJ, we are supposed to believe that the CEO of the Microsoft Applications Company and his attorneys—all of whom would be cautioned by the once-unitary company's antitrust loss in the May 1998 case—would order the company to launch a massive assault against all the rest of the Linux office suite business. This assault, upon completion, would leave the Microsoft Applications Company with 90 percent of the Linux office suite market, and barriers to entry would be so strong that no significant competitor could arise. Would the CEO of Microsoft Applications Company tell his employees, "Don't worry about antitrust, folks. We'll never get sued. Building a Linux suites monopoly is exactly what the Department of Justice wanted us to do in the year 2000. We can be confident they'll never change their mind and sue us for monopolizing this new market."

Absurd, isn't it? But say the Applications Company goes on to produce Office for Linux and to develop all versions of Office as middleware. Assume further that the new products are highly profitable, and that the Department of Justice leaves the Applications Company alone. What would the Applications Company do next?

Perhaps the company would enter the server market, for which Unix holds the largest market share. (Windows NT/2000 is second.) The Applications Company would announce the introduction of "Microsoft Unix." The new Microsoft Unix would include scores of special extensions that make Office for Unix work better when running with a Microsoft Unix server than with a Unix server from Sun, IBM, or other Unix companies. To make matters worse, the Microsoft Applications Company might give away Microsoft Unix for free, and include a free copy of Microsoft Unix with every copy of Unix Office.

One can almost hear the caterwauling from Novell, Sun, IBM, and Oracle as Microsoft Unix begins to take market share from them. These companies—the same ones who lobbied for the current anti-Microsoft lawsuit—will run back to the DOJ, which will launch an antitrust investigation of Microsoft's use of its "Unix office suite applications monopoly" to attempt to create a "Unix operating system monopoly."

RAISING THE PRICE OF WINDOWS

What would the Microsoft "Windows Company" be doing while the Applications Company pondered whether to create Office for Linux?

If Windows and Office really are monopolies, then separating them would hurt rather than benefit consumers. So long as both programs are under one corporate roof, Microsoft has an incentive to cut prices for one to boost sales of the other—for example, to keep Windows prices low in order to create more customers for Office. (Economists call this the theory of "complementary monopolies" or "double marginalization.") With the two separated, the Windows company and the Office company would each have an incentive to maximize revenue without regard to the other's sales. The economic assumptions made by DOJ expert Franklin Fisher suggest the price of Windows would triple, raising the retail price to over $500.[26] Another study estimates that worldwide consumers would spend between $125 billion and $310 billion more over the next three years if both companies abandoned Microsoft's low-price strategy.[27]

In the history of antitrust, we've seen this happen before. When antitrust law was used to break up Standard Oil into regional companies, consumers were not given more choices or lower prices, since the regional companies maintained their local monopolies.[28] The real effect of the Standard Oil case was to diminish the bargaining power of oil companies vis-a-vis railroads. Once Standard Oil was broken up, rail shipping prices rose and the retail price of petroleum went up. Perverse consequences, as will be shown in the next chapter, have been the rule and not the exception in the history of antitrust.

The Department of Justice and its economists concede the problem, but argue the price increase will be offset in the long term by all the benefits flowing from Office for Linux, including Office's metamorphosis into middleware. In other words, the main point of the breakup is to triple the price of Windows as the necessary consumer sacrifice for the possibility that the Applications Company will create Office for Linux. This is, once again, the conceit of wanna-be industrial planners. It would probably be less costly for consumers if the federal government simply imposed a $50 per-unit tax on Windows, granted itself a license for Office, and used the tax money to fund a Federal Bureau of Unix Office Creation.

That Office for Unix, like the unicorn, may be purely mythological does not seem to deter the DOJ's deep thinkers.

---

[26]Richard Schmalensee, Defendant's Offer of Proof, *U.S. v. Microsoft*, May 24, 2000, ¶ 3.

[27]Stan J. Liebowitz, *An Expensive Pig in a Poke: Estimating the Cost of the District Court's Proposed Breakup of Microsoft* (Washington, DC: Association for Competitive Technology, 2000).

[28]See Dominick T. Armentano, *Antitrust and Monopoly: Anatomy of a Policy Failure* (Oakland, CA: Independent Institute, second edition, 1990), pages 55-84; Jim Johnston, "Dolly Parton, John D. Rockefeller, and Bill Gates," *Intellectual Ammunition*, January/February 2000, pages 1, 3.

BREAKING WINDOWS

While the portion of Judge Jackson's order calling for a breakup of Microsoft gets most of the attention, other provisions of the order would severely undermine the quality of Windows. The order gives the Department of Justice what it has sought for years: veto power over changes in Windows.

Disclosing Internal Interfaces

The Windows Company and the Applications Company would be restricted from working cooperatively on projects where the operating system and the applications must work together, such as toolbars or clipboards. Any discussion of such applications would have to be "simultaneously published" to the whole computer industry. This would be particularly burdensome in the Personal Digital Assistant market (where Microsoft is a very distant second), since attempts to improve the Windows CE system for PDAs need to be coordinated with applications improvements for PDAs.

Worse, Microsoft would be required to disclose the internal interfaces for Windows. Currently, a software application interacts with Windows by calling on an Application Programming Interface (API). The API then interacts with the rest of Windows to accomplish whatever the application wants to have done (*e.g.*, print a document, activate the modem, display a dialog box, make a sound).

When Windows receives a command from outside the OS (*e.g.*, from a software application or a Java applet), Windows performs a security check to make sure the order is authorized. Windows would not accept, for example, an order from a Java applet that said "erase the entire Registry."[29]

For intra-Windows orders (one part of the OS giving an order to a different part of the OS), security checks are not performed. To require checks would significantly slow down the OS.[30] But if the Windows internal interfaces were exposed to the whole world, then security checks would become mandatory. Software applications would try to call on the internal interfaces, just as they currently call on APIs. Virus writers, too, would have access to much deeper

---

[29]The Windows Registry contains configuration specifications and settings for software.

[30]Microsoft Corporation's Offer of Proof, proposed testimony of Professor John Bennett, *U.S. vs. Microsoft*, May 24, 2000, at ¶ 4.

and more vulnerable levels of Windows.

To maintain backwards compatibility—so that, for example, a program written for Windows 95 can still run on Windows 98—Microsoft must keep some APIs static. Thus, when the application program calls for a Windows 95-type API, Windows 98 can supply one. Should internal interfaces be exposed, they too would have to remain static, thus massively impeding the development of new versions of Windows.

It is difficult to justify this invasion of Microsoft's intellectual property rights and outright sabotage of Windows on the grounds, expressed by Judge Jackson, that all this is necessary to "level the playing field" between Windows applications developers and developers writing for other operating systems. Microsoft sells products in 21 of the 99 different software categories monitored by the research firm International Data Corp.[31] In only four of the 99 categories does Microsoft's market share exceed 36 percent.

No Innovation Without Government Permission?

During the litigation over the 1995 Consent Decree, the Department of Justice asked for an order that Microsoft could change nothing about Windows—not even to fix a bug—without prior assent from the DOJ. Investment analyst Scott McAdams explained why the federal government and the state attorneys general were never able to achieve a compromise with Microsoft: "They [Microsoft] want to retain the right to design products the way they want to. The government never wanted to concede that."[32] In 2000, Judge Jackson restricted Microsoft's integration of "middleware" products into Windows.

Suppose that Judge Jackson's prior restraint remedy is upheld and that, in a few years, the Windows Company decides to add strong public key encryption to the Windows operating system. Public key encryption is an excellent choice for inclusion; like email before Windows 95, encryption is a very useful tool, but it is not widely used because most people find it too much trouble to set up and operate. Without a large enough installed base of users, the people who do install encryption on their personal computers have few people to whom they can send encrypted email. Windows encryption would solve the problem in an instant; there would be a large base of users, and network effects would start

---

[31]"After the Verdict, Companies Consider the Impact," *Wall Street Journal*, April 4, 2000, page A12.

[32]Bill Virgin, "'Win at All Costs' Sowed Seeds of a Bitter Harvest," *Seattle Post-Intelligencer*, June 8, 2000.

working in favor of ubiquitous encryption. Full integration into the Windows operating system could make encryption operate seamlessly and almost effortlessly for the consumer (just as today's Windows consumers have no idea how to use the Terminal Control Protocol/Internet Protocol stacks that Windows takes care of during Web browsing).

The encryption integration would be a good deal for consumers, but it would be vigorously opposed by the DOJ, which has been lobbying Congress, with little success, to stop public key encryption. Judge Jackson's order would give the DOJ authority, without permission from Congress, to stop Windows from integrating strong encryption. Of course, the DOJ would claim only an unselfish concern for the small encryption companies that would be wiped out by Microsoft leveraging its OS monopoly into an encryption monopoly.

Although predicting exactly what kind of new Windows capabilities the DOJ would prohibit is impossible, it is clear the DOJ does not mean to let Bill Gates add whatever he wants. A broken Microsoft would find it nearly impossible to pursue such projects as Gates' plans for Next Generation Windows Services, which attempt to integrate new features such as speech and handwriting recognition, and would be designed to run on PCs, PDAs, and other platforms.

The DOJ order would probably create more competition in the long run, but only by preventing future improvements to Windows. Eventually, some other company would invent a Windows-compatible operating system, and that company would not be stifled by a cadre of DOJ attorneys, at least not until the new company is marked by regulators with the scarlet "M-for-monopoly."

Interestingly, the requirement that Windows add nothing without asking the government first is touted for its virtue in avoiding regulation. If prior restraint is not regulation, what is?

BRIEFLY STATED . . .

Judge Thomas Penfield Jackson found Microsoft guilty of a victimless crime. The government's own experts testified that no harm to consumers had occurred, and the government produced no consumers who testified they were harmed. Extensive investigation of Microsoft's internal communications documents showed no intent to prevent or obstruct innovation by other companies.

Lacking such proof of the commission of a crime, Judge Jackson conjured up a variety of minor and largely hypothetical inconveniences that *may have* resulted from Microsoft's business practices. These "harms"—occupying more space on a customer's hard drive and the like—simply do not reach the level of significance necessary for federal intervention.

The most significant remedy imposed against Microsoft has nothing to do with the company's supposed illegal conduct. The proposed breakup of the company into Operating System and Applications Companies goes far beyond whatever would be necessary to stop anti-competitive behavior. The order is radical (without precedent) and seems to reflect the resentment of a humiliated judge and DOJ, rather than an attempt at attaining justice.

Unsurprisingly, the punishments that would bear no relation to the alleged crimes would fail to produce the desired outcome. Consumers would not be helped. Competition would not emerge. Innovation, far from being encouraged, would be squashed under the thumb of DOJ bureaucrats.

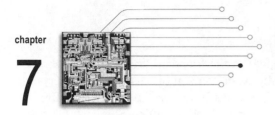

Learning
from the Past

T his chapter performs a quick survey of past responses to emerging monopolies and their consequences.[1] The first history looks at "antitrust's greatest hits," three major antitrust cases that helped create much of the vocabulary used in the current debate. Misinterpretation of these cases lies behind the claim that Microsoft, unless punished, regulated, or broken up, will achieve a "chokehold on the Internet."

The second history is of the transportation industry. It records a case where one part of an industry—passenger and freight railroads—was heavily regulated in the name of avoiding "ruinous competition" while another—automobiles—was not. The record plainly shows that heavy-handed regulation crippled the railroad industry, creating a legacy of inefficiency and bankruptcy that ended, for the freight railroads, only with the advent of deregulation in 1980, and continues to this day for passenger railroads. The automobile industry, by contrast, is characterized by rapid growth, innovation, competition, and responsiveness to consumers.

The third history looks at the anti-Microsoft campaign, now in its fifth year. Few of the claims and predictions made at the beginning of the case have stood even this modest test of time.

---

[1] Joseph Bast contributed to this chapter.

ANTITRUST'S GREATEST HITS

U.S. v. Standard Oil
(N.J.) (1911)

The Microsoft case is often compared to the Standard Oil case. For example, Gary Reback, a lawyer for some Microsoft competitors, has claimed, "the only thing J.D. Rockefeller did that Bill Gates hasn't done is use dynamite against his competitors."[2] Judge Jackson also compared Microsoft to Standard Oil.[3] The analogy is apt.[4] Standard Oil was personally selected as a target by President Theodore Roosevelt because its founder and CEO, John D. Rockefeller, was defiant rather than submissive when the federal government began to challenge his business practices.

Like Microsoft, Standard Oil was pilloried for using business practices considered legitimate when used by other companies. Since Standard Oil was a high-volume customer, railroads gave it special discounts in exchange for planning shipments in ways that enabled railroads to use their lines and railcars most efficiently. Standard Oil's competitors complained bitterly about these discounts (called "rebates"), which the railroads kept secret from other oil companies.

Standard Oil, like Microsoft, may have harmed competitors but helped consumers. John D. Rockefeller and his chemists developed 300 different by-products from oil and created production and distribution processes far more efficient than those of its competitors, allowing it for a brief period of time to underprice and eventually buy out many of its direct competitors. The parallels with Microsoft, again, are obvious.

Standard Oil began in 1870 as an Ohio company with a 4 percent market share. Kerosene cost 30 cents a gallon. By 1897, Standard Oil had driven the price down to under 6 cents per gallon and many of its less-efficient competitors were out of business—including companies whose inferior grades of kerosene were prone to explosion and whose dangerous products had depressed the

---

[2]John Heilemann, "The Truth, the Whole Truth and Nothing but the Truth," *Wired*, November 2000, page 264.

[3]*United States v. Microsoft*, trial transcript, February 22, 2000, afternoon session, page 42.

[4]The following account is a brief summary of longer accounts appearing in Dominick Armentano, *Antitrust and Monopoly: Anatomy of a Policy Failure* (Oakland, CA: Independent Institute, second edition, 1990), pages 55-84, and by the same author, *The Myths of Antitrust* (New York, NY: Arlington House, 1990); Matthew Josephson, *The Robber Barons: The Great American Capitalists, 1861-1901* (New York, NY: Harcourt, Brace and Company, 1934), pages 109-120, 159-163, 270-289; Burton Folsom Jr., *The Myth of the Robber Barons* (Herndon, VA: Young America's Foundation, 1996); and Richard B. McKenzie, *Trust on Trial: How the Microsoft Case is Reframing the Rules of Competition* (Cambridge, MA: Perseus Books, 2000), pages 57-58.

demand for kerosene. Rockefeller also did for petroleum what he did for kerosene. In a single decade, from 1880 to 1890, Rockefeller's consolidations helped drive petroleum prices down 61 percent while increasing output 393 percent.[5]

Standard Oil used resources with legendary efficiency, introducing many new labor-saving devices to its factories and locating sophisticated facilities at key points in its distribution system. Yet Rockefeller paid wages well above the market level, believing that high wages and good working conditions would save money in the long run by averting strikes and encouraging loyalty.

Rockefeller eventually built Standard Oil of New Jersey into a trust composed of 18 companies operating under a single board of directors. As the author of a recent biography of John D. Rockefeller observes, "the trust blanketed oil fields with efficient pipelines and pioneered marketing by tank wagons. It was dreaded more for its low, predatory pricing than for fleecing consumers."[6]

It is difficult to overstate the benefits that Standard Oil's innovation and efficiency brought to its customers. Before Standard Oil revolutionized oil derivatives by lowering their prices and improving their quality, the high prices and limited supplies of whale oil and candles prevented all but the wealthy from being able to work or entertain after dark. Thanks to Standard Oil, families could illuminate their homes for just one cent per hour.

The federal government filed suit against Standard Oil in 1906 for violating the Sherman Act, and the company was convicted in 1909. The conviction was affirmed by the U.S. Supreme Court in 1911. Standard Oil, according to the courts, evinced an "intent and purpose to exclude others," as shown (with irony apparently overlooked by the courts) by Standard Oil's many mergers, acquisitions, and business alliances. No evidence of consumer harm was brought forward during the trial and a case against the legality of Standard's specific actions, as opposed to its supposed intent, was never offered. Dominick T. Armentano summarized the decision like this:

> No economic analysis of Standard Oil's conduct and performance in the period under consideration was made by the Court to determine whether its business activities were reasonable. Standard was convicted and partially dissolved in 1911, but an economic analysis of its conduct

---

[5]David R. Henderson, "The Case Against the Microsoft Suit," *Red Herring*, August 1998, www.redherring.com.

[6]Ron Chernow, "How to Save a Titan," *New York Times*, April 19, 1998.

had little, if anything, to do with that decision.[7]

For several decades following the Standard Oil verdict, the case was viewed by economists and legal scholars as a classic example of "predatory pricing," an attempt by a monopolist to drive competitors out of the market by cutting prices, so as to raise prices at a later time. But just as the threat of new entry into the OS, browser, and applications markets has kept Microsoft from ever exercising this "monopoly power," so did new sources of competition keep Standard Oil from raising its prices. A famous study of the matter by John S. McGee, published in 1958, found:

> Judging from the Record, Standard Oil did not use predatory price discrimination to drive out competing refiners, nor did its pricing practice have that effect. Whereas there may be a very few cases in which retail kerosene peddlers or dealers went out of business after or during price cutting, there is no real proof that Standard's pricing policies were responsible. I am convinced that Standard did not systematically, if ever, use local price cutting in retailing, or anywhere else, to reduce competition.[8]

Notably, neither the federal district court nor the U.S. Supreme Court found that Standard Oil's practices made kerosene prices higher than they otherwise would have been.[9]

John D. Rockefeller was a deeply religious man who gave some $540 million to charity before his death in 1937 (about $6 billion in today's dollars), more than any other person in history *except Bill Gates.*[10] Yet his public image was smeared by "exposés" written by two supposedly progressive authors who happened to be related to Rockefeller's competitors: Henry Demarest Lloyd, the cousin of a disgruntled oil man, who wrote *Wealth Against Commonwealth* (1894); and Ida Tarbell, daughter of a Pennsylvania oil producer and sister of the treasurer of the Pure Oil Company, who slammed

---

[7]Dominick T. Armentano, *Antitrust and Monopoly, supra* note 4, page 73.

[8]John S. McGee, "Predatory Price Cutting: The Standard Oil (N.J.) Case," *Journal of Law and Economics*, Vol. 1, October 1958, page 169.

[9]*Standard Oil Co. of New Jersey v. United States*, 221 U.S. 1 (1911), *affirming*, 173 F. 177 (E.D. Mo. 1909).

[10]Jean Strouse, "How to Give Away $21.8 billion," *New York Times Magazine*, April 16, 2000, page 58. According to Strouse, Rockefeller's giving in today's dollars is "less than a third of the Gates total so far."

Rockefeller in *The History of the Standard Oil Company* (1904)[11] and in a series of magazine articles. Those articles helped persuade the Roosevelt administration to target Standard Oil for a major antitrust suit.

Technological change made the Standard Oil decision obsolete by the time it was resolved. The oil business was opening fields in states such as Kansas, Oklahoma, Louisiana, and California, and especially in Texas, where Rockefeller had failed to invest.[12] All of those fields were far away from the Ohio/Pennsylvania/New Jersey corridor that was the base of Standard Oil's power.

Also, the national kerosene market declined as home lighting shifted from kerosene lamps to coal-generated electricity, and as fuel oil replaced coal and wood as the major fuel for home heating. In 1899, kerosene had accounted for 58 percent of all refined petroleum sales, and fuel oil for 15 percent. By 1914, kerosene had plunged to 25 percent, and fuel oil had risen to 48 percent.[13]

The major source of growth in the energy business after the turn of the century was demand for gasoline for the nation's fledgling fleet of automobiles. Rockefeller was slow to switch from kerosene to gasoline, and with only 11 percent of the nation's oil production in 1911, Standard Oil could never hope to achieve the dominance in gasoline it had earned with kerosene. Throughout the energy business, new technologies and new efficiencies were creating new and stronger competitors from industries previously distinct from the oil industry. Those competitors were far more powerful than the kerosene companies Rockefeller had defeated decades before.

Some writers note that in the years after Standard Oil was broken into smaller regional companies, the stock prices of those smaller companies rose, leading to speculation that breaking up Microsoft might have a similar positive effect on the value of Microsoft stock. This, too, is a misreading of the Standard Oil case. Increasing stock prices were experienced by nearly all oil companies following the breakup of Standard Oil, almost certainly due to rising demand and technological breakthroughs and not the breakup.[14] Nor did the breakup

---

[11]Available online at www.history.rochester.edu/fuels/tarbell/main.htm.

[12]Robert W. Crandall, "If It Ain't Broke, Don't Break It Up," *Wall Street Journal*, June 14, 2000, page A26.

[13]Dominick T. Armentano, *Antitrust and Monopoly, supra* note 4, pages 66-67, citing J. Stanley Clark, *The Oil Century* (Norman, OK: University of Oklahoma Press, 1958), page 127.

[14]Atin Basu Choudhany, Robert Tollison and William F. Shugart II, "Titan Agonistes: Wealth Effects in the Standard Oil Case," paper presented at a meeting of the Southern Economic Association, New Orleans, November 22, 1999.

have any discernible impact on oil production or oil prices.[15]

The government's victory in the antitrust case against Standard Oil had a long-term effect on the oil industry that is seldom discussed by those who see parallels with the Microsoft case. Only six years after losing the antitrust case, Standard Oil dramatically changed its attitude toward Washington DC, moving from hostility or avoidance to what may be called a very warm embrace. Its CEO, A.C. Bedford, went to Washington to serve as chairman of the War Services Committee, an agency created to mobilize the nation's supplies of gasoline and diesel fuel for military use during World War I.

After the war, federal control never retreated, transforming what once had been "a virtual textbook example of a free and competitive market" into "what had previously been unobtainable: a governmentally sanctioned cartel in oil."[16] The legacies of this transformation include higher prices for consumers and the "energy crisis" of the 1970s. Deregulation in the 1980s under President Ronald Reagan finally restored competition and innovation to the industry.[17]

The Standard Oil case teaches some important lessons about competition, innovation, and antitrust law. We see how antitrust law has difficulty dealing with highly innovative companies. We witness the vagueness of antitrust law, which allows prosecution on the basis of alleged criminal intent rather than specific actions. Enforcement of antitrust law in the Standard Oil case ultimately did not benefit consumers or investors. The antitrust case against Standard Oil laid the groundwork for later collusion between industry and government that brought about many of the very ills "progressive" proponents of antitrust alleged were the result of monopoly. Only the repeal of regulations, once justified by the now-discredited "predatory pricing" theory, allowed the industry to once again become innovative and competitive.

U.S. v. Aluminum Company of America (1945)

In 1937, the U.S. government filed suit in the Federal District Court for the Southern District of New York against the Aluminum Company of America

---

[15]Robert W. Crandall, "If It Ain't Broke, Don't Break It Up," *supra* note 11.

[16]Dominick T. Armentano, *Antitrust and Monopoly, supra* note 4, pages 73-74.

[17]See Robert Bradley, *Oil, Gas, and Government: The U.S. Experience* (Washington, DC: Cato Institute, 1996), for a complete telling of the story.

alleging over one hundred violations of antitrust law.[18] The government lost the case and appealed. The matter was finally decided eight years later, in 1945, with what was essentially a split decision. This case is remarkable because it held that a company could be prosecuted under antitrust laws for being *too efficient* and *responding too quickly to consumer demand.*

The Aluminum Company of America (later, Alcoa) grew out of the Pittsburgh Reduction Company, founded in 1887 by Charles Hall, the man who discovered and patented the technology for producing commercial quantities of aluminum. At the time, aluminum ingots sold for $5 a pound. By the time the Department of Justice sued Alcoa in 1937, the price was down to 22 cents per pound.[19]

Alcoa dominated its industry from the start. It not only invented nearly all of the tools and techniques required to lower production costs and raise the quality of the aluminum it produced, it also played a major role in creating markets for the new metal by going head to head with manufacturers of other metals for use in fabricating wire, cookware, tableware, medical instruments, automobile engines and body components, building materials, and many other applications.

While many companies entered the business of fabricating products out of aluminum and collecting and recycling used aluminum, none attempted to compete with Alcoa by producing virgin aluminum ingots. The reason was not that Alcoa restricted access to inputs such as electricity or aluminum bauxite, both of which the courts ruled were available to potential competitors in ample supply. Nor, after 1910, was access to the manufacturing techniques patented by Alcoa denied to potential competitors, since the patents had expired. As Dominick Armentano summarized the situation, "users of ingot or sheet, and ultimately the consumers of fabricated products made from aluminum by Alcoa, were being served at degrees of excellence, prices, and profit rates that no one could equal or exceed."[20]

The lower court found Alcoa innocent of all counts of anti-competitive behavior, even while acknowledging that Alcoa was a monopolist controlling 90 percent of the market for virgin aluminum ingot (the other 10 percent being imports). District Court Judge Francis G. Caffey reasoned that the Sherman Act forbade activity aimed at monopolizing markets, but did not outlaw the common

---

[18]Major sources for this discussion include Dominick T. Armentano, *Antitrust and Monopoly, supra* note 4, pages 100-112; Fred S. McChesney and William F. Shughart II, editors, *The Causes and Consequences of Antitrust: The Public-Choice Perspective* (Chicago, IL: University of Chicago Press, 1995), pages 43-44.

[19]Dominick T. Armentano, *Antitrust and Monopoly, supra* note 4, page 102.

[20]*Ibid.*, page 103.

business practices of companies that held dominant market shares due simply to the absence of competitors.

The special Appeals Court that heard the government's appeal agreed with Judge Caffey that the government had failed to show Alcoa engaged in anti-competitive behavior or charged higher prices than it should. However, Judge Learned Hand, writing for the majority, held that Alcoa's *de facto* monopoly was sufficient grounds to constitute a violation of antitrust law. The Judge wrote:

> It was not inevitable that it [Alcoa] should always anticipate increases in the demand for ingot and be prepared to supply them. Nothing compelled it to keep doubling and redoubling its capacity before others entered the field. It insists that it never excluded competitors; but we can think of no more effective exclusion than progressively to embrace each new opportunity as it opened, and to face every newcomer with new capacity already geared into a great organization, having the advantage of experience, trade connection and the elite of personnel.[21]

The Alcoa case shows how, in the Orwellian world of antitrust, a company that holds a monopoly share of a narrowly defined market can be found guilty of being too efficient or of moving too quickly to satisfy consumers' demands. One is reminded of stories that police sometimes pull over drivers late at night who drive at exactly the speed limit and stay in the middle of their lanes, since this kind of careful conduct late at night may be evidence of overcompensation by a drunken driver. This is the sort of bizarre result that comes from enforcing laws that criminalize a state of mind rather than a particular action.

Having found no evidence of specific actions that were illegal, the court could hardly include in its remedies restrictions on Alcoa's current business practices. Nor, since the firm's outstanding efficiency and service to consumers were recognized by the court, did it seem right to break up the company. Instead, the court settled for prohibiting the company from bidding for government aluminum plants built to meet World War II military needs. Those assets were subsequently sold to Reynolds Metal and Kaiser Aluminum.

In 1948, Alcoa and the federal government asked the New York District Court to reconsider the 1945 decision, Alcoa because it sought to be relieved of the scarlet "M-for-monopoly" that effectively criminalized its common business

---

[21]*United States v. Aluminum Company of America*, 148 F. 2d 416, 430-431 (2d Cir., 1945).

practices, and the government to force Alcoa to divest some of its holdings.[22] The district court, under the direction of a different judge than in 1937, once again found the government's case without merit, and this time ruled further that Alcoa was no longer a monopolist.

So, where are they now? In 2000, Alcoa acquired Reynolds Metals Co., then the third-largest aluminum maker in the U.S. According to a report in the *Wall Street Journal*, Alcoa still isn't acting like a monopolist:

> Alcoa said it was still on track to cut $1.1 billion in annualized cost savings by January. But that goal excludes the rising costs of natural gas and fuel, which rose $70 million in the first nine months of 2000. So far, the company said it has achieved $924 million in annualized cost savings.[23]

U.S. v. AT&T (1981)

Besides the *Standard Oil* case, the case most touted by advocates of the Microsoft prosecution is *United States v. AT&T*, the case that led to the breakup of AT&T.[24] Although both cases involve information technology, there are important differences.

To begin with, AT&T was the kind of monopoly Adam Smith would have recognized: The company had lobbied for, and won, government protection against competition. It maintained its market share thanks partly to an array of legal prohibitions on other companies entering the market for any part of the telephone services market, be it local or long-distance service or even telephones and other equipment that could be attached to a phone line.

Peter Huber described the situation as follows:

> Bell itself wanted to consolidate its dominant position and legitimize its monopoly. Theodore Vail [the first president of AT&T] spoke publicly in favor of regulation, sounding a theme ("cream skimming") that would

---

[22]*United States v. Aluminum Company of America*, 91 F. Supp. 333 (1948).

[23]Robert Guy Matthews, "Alcoa's Third-Quarter Net Income Climbed 42%," *Wall Street Journal*, October 6, 2000, page A14.

[24]*United States v. AT&T*, 524 F. Supp. 1336 (D.D.C. 1981); *United States v. AT&T*, 552 F. Supp. 131 (D.D.C. 1982).

become a Bell rallying cry for the next half-century. "If there is to be state control and regulation," Vail argued, "there should also be state protection to a corporation striving to serve the whole community . . . from aggressive competition which covers only that part which is profitable."[25]

Obviously, Microsoft has not called for similar protections from its competitors, nor is it today similarly protected.

A second difference is that the AT&T divestiture simply undid acquisitions from decades before, in which AT&T had swallowed local phone operating companies. Microsoft, by contrast, has never merged. All of its growth has been internal.

A third difference in the two cases is that AT&T had capital and employees dispersed all over the United States to service its customers. AT&T could therefore divest itself of local telephone companies, which were then organized into seven "Baby Bells" to provide regional phone service. Microsoft, with its capital far more centralized and with much less need to have people "on the ground" in geographically defined areas (except for sales), would be far more adversely affected than AT&T by such a legal order.

The settlement that led to the AT&T breakup also liberated AT&T from a 1956 antitrust consent decree preventing the company from entering and competing in non-regulated businesses (*e.g.*, data processing). In exchange for this *deregulation*, AT&T voluntarily acceded to divestiture. Thus, the AT&T breakup was a consensual step towards deregulating a part of the economy that had long been regulated under the public utility model. The Microsoft case, once again, is much different, since the digital economy has been the freest part of the American economy. A Microsoft breakup order would represent a major increase in government intervention in this part of the economy.

Finally, the AT&T breakup was only partly successful. One part of the voluntary breakup created a competitor in the long-distance market, free to introduce new technologies. This part of the breakup seems to have been successful, with AT&T moving into cable, wireless, and other kinds of data transmission arenas and competing with a variety of global competitors.[26] But much of the old AT&T was left behind as the local Bell companies, which were forbidden to manufacture telephone equipment or design new telephone products. The theory was that preventing these Baby Bells from entering the arena of equipment manufacture and design would prevent them from using

---

[25]Peter Huber, *Orwell's Revenge: The 1984 Palimpsest* (New York, NY: Free Press, 1994), page 267.

[26]Jason Krause, "Ma Bell's Future On the Line," *The Industry Standard,* October 2, 2000, pages 58-60.

profits from the local telephone service business to subsidize new businesses.[27] The case has been made, however, that the arrangement has created regional local phone monopolies that have been slow to innovate or to allow competitors to gain access to their captive markets.[28]

Judge Greene's supervision of the telephone companies continued from the 1982 entry of the Consent Decree until 1996, when an exasperated Congress dissolved the Consent Decree. In the intervening period, 250 applications for waivers (usually by local Bell companies wanting to sell or license a new technology) sat on Judge Greene's docket for an average of four years. The Department of Justice processed 360 waivers, taking an average of three years for each request.[29]

Antitrust is sometimes said to be superior to formal regulation, in that antitrust does not require continuing government oversight of the company's business. But the AT&T case demonstrates that enforcement of antitrust laws can generate as much or more government intervention. Like the Standard Oil case, the AT&T case reveals a pattern of government intervention expanding over time, first to manage prices and avoid "unhealthy" competition, then approving and disapproving of mergers and acquisitions, and ultimately ruling on whether to allow innovations in products and services. This is not a "policy . . . employed by a society that wishes to use the competitive market, rather than powerful private or public bodies, to regulate most economic activity."[30] Rather, it is a prescription for a gradual and unlimited expansion of government control over markets.

PLANES, TRAINS, AND AUTOMOBILES

Following the history of a particular industry can reveal the consequences of regulatory choices. The transportation industry is an especially appropriate case because some of its critics claim Microsoft should be subject to the same rules as apply to common carriers, of which trains are the classic case.[31] The parallel

---

[27]James L. Gattuso, "Judge Greene of the 21st Century?" C/Spin, May 2, 2000, www.cei.org.

[28]Adam D. Thierer, "What's Next for Telecommunications Deregulation?" Backgrounder #1145, The Heritage Foundation, October 28, 1997.

[29]Association for Competitive Technology, Breakup and Compulsory Licensing, Remedies or Bad Medicine (February 18, 1999), www.actonline.org/pubs/white_paper.asp.

[30]George Stigler, The Organization of Industry (Homewood, IL: Richard D. Irwin, Inc., 1968), page 297.

[31]Richard A. Epstein compares trains and Microsoft in chapter 10 of Principles for a Free Society: Reconciling Individual Liberty with the Common Good (Reading, MA: Perseus Books, 1998), pages 279-318.

is even closer because a century ago railroads faced some of the same decisions facing the information technology industry today. History shows they chose poorly.

Trains were the new technology of the latter part of the nineteenth century. They promised to "change everything," from how products were made and sold to where cities would be built, from the dissemination of information to intimate details of private life. The impact on the U.S. economy of railroads, beginning in the 1840s, was every bit as dramatic as the impact of the Internet today. The expansion of railroads from 1850 until World War I was, in Howard Mumford Jones's memorable phrase, "an epic chapter in an epic time."[32]

The railroads made possible speedy, safe, and reliable transportation of passengers and goods in a nation that had previously relied on a loose network of rutted dirt roads. Prior to railroads, it was prohibitively expensive for most American goods to be sold more than 200 miles from where they were produced. By expanding the size of markets, railroads made possible a greater division of labor, and hence greater productivity gains.[33] Once the railroad network was established, horseshoes could be made by the tens of thousands in urban factories and distributed all over the United States, or even sent to ports on the coasts for export to other countries—rather than be made one at a time by a village blacksmith. Local markets in farm goods merged into regional, then national, and finally international markets.

Railroads were a boon to the producers of almost every product. They dramatically lowered shipping costs and delivery times, and thus fueled growing demand for products. They opened up vast expanses of the countryside to development, boosting demand for all of the products needed for city-building. Railroads also allowed producers to profit from local or regional interruptions of supply; allowing, for example, a farmer in Illinois to ship wheat to Georgia when a drought had ruined Southern crops.

Consumers flourished as well. Railroads broke up the local and regional monopolies often held by local merchants. The only dry goods store in a small town was suddenly faced with competition from national catalog merchants such as Sears Roebuck or Montgomery Ward, which could ship their products directly to consumers rather than going through local merchants. Retailers had

---

[32]Howard Mumford Jones, *The Age of Energy: Varieties of American Experience, 1865-1915* (New York, NY: The Viking Press), page 150.

[33]The relationship between the size of markets and the division of labor was one of the central themes of Adam Smith's *An Inquiry into the Nature and Causes of the Wealth of Nations* (Indianapolis, IN: Liberty Classics, 1981 [1776]); see especially Book 1, Chapter 3. One implication of Smith's insight is that markets may naturally tend toward monopoly, a problem elegantly discussed by George Stigler in a 1951 article, reprinted as chapter 12 in *The Organization of Industry*, *supra* note 29, pages 129-141.

to respond by redefining their market niches, often by specializing in providing a superior selection of a smaller number of goods or services than were offered by national companies. Like the Internet, the railroads helped connect buyers and sellers previously separated by time, space, and intermediaries.[34]

Railroad
Regulation

Railroads were regulated sooner and more extensively than any other sector of the industrial economy. Three reasons account for this. The railroads demanded and received government subsidies for laying track across the country: some 130 million acres of public land; right-of-way through public and private lands and freedom to use materials on the public domain; donations of cash, equipment, materials, and labor; public purchases of railroad stock, often at inflated prices; exemption from local, state, and federal taxes; and more. The total value of these subsidies was estimated in 1971 to be in the range of $600 million to $1,500 million.[35]

In return for these subsidies and favors, the railroads agreed to carry freight for the government at reduced rates, which they did until 1946. According to one expert, "It is possible that the government by that time had saved as much on transport costs as it had spent on public aid."[36] From the beginning, railroads found themselves enmeshed in deals and complex agreements with local, state, and federal government officials and regulators, a situation that would often be used to justify government interventions in the industry.

The second reason for the extensive regulation of railroads was the swift recognition that railroads had the power to make or break individual businesses and even cities. Courts ruled that the rates and business practices of railroads could be regulated by state and national agencies because their services were "affected with a public interest." In a major 1877 case concerning grain elevators in Illinois, *Munn v. Illinois*, the Supreme Court ruled:

Property does become clothed with a public interest when used in a

---

[34]John Steele Gordon, "The Golden Spike," *Forbes ASAP*, February 21, 2000, pages 118-122.

[35]Clair Wilcox, *Public Policies Toward Business* (Homewood, IL: Richard D. Irwin, Inc., fourth edition, 1971), page 368. Assuming Wilcox's estimates are in 1969 dollars, the inflation-adjusted values in 1999 dollars would be $2.7 billion and $6.8 billion.

[36]*Ibid.*, pages 368-369.

manner to make it of public consequence, and affect the community at large. When, therefore, one devotes his property to a use in which the public has an interest, he, in effect, grants the public an interest in that use, and must submit to be controlled by the public for the common good.[37]

Munn v. Illinois laid the legal foundation for states to regulate railroads and other "natural monopolies" such as water, gas, electric, and telephone companies. A Supreme Court decision a half-century later essentially held that *all* businesses are in some way "affected with a public interest" and therefore subject to state and federal regulation, provided that the "laws passed are seen to have a reasonable relation to a proper legislative purpose, and are neither arbitrary nor discriminatory. . . ."[38]

The third reason for the early regulation of railroads was the economic nature of the industry. Railroads, like the information technology industry, are characterized by large up-front investments and fixed costs (tracks and rolling stock in the first case, research and development budgets in the latter), and relatively low variable costs (the cost of providing service to one more shipper, or of producing and selling one more copy of software). Since fixed costs are distributed over the number of units sold, the average cost per unit falls as sales volume rises. So long as there is excess capacity in such industries, companies have strong incentives to increase their volume of sales even at prices below their average per-unit costs, so long as each additional unit is sold at a price that covers its variable costs.[39]

The tendency to charge prices below average cost, combined with an oversupply of railroad capacity (due partly to the aforementioned subsidies), led to fierce price competition during the 1870s. For many economists and legal scholars writing before the 1980s, this episode was the principal historical example of "ruinous competition." For example, a standard graduate textbook on regulation published in 1971 contains the following account:

> During the years of railroad building, little thought had been given to the possible need for regulation. Several roads were built in every section of the country, and it was assumed that competition between

---

[37]*Munn v. Illinois*, 94 U.S. 113 (1877).

[38]*Nebbia v. New York*, 291 U.S. 502 (1934).

[39]William J. Baumol *et al.*, "The Role of Cost in the Minimum Pricing of Railroad Services," *Journal of Business*, Vol. 35, No. 4 (October 1962), pages 358-366; William Vickrey, "Some Implications of Marginal Cost Pricing for Public Utilities," *American Economic Review*, Vol. 45, No. 2 (May 1955), pages 605-620.

them would protect the public interest. But competition proved, instead, to be ruinous. And it led, shortly, to collusive agreements among the railroad companies. The level of rates was raised, and discrimination was practiced between persons, between products, and between communities. The public attitude toward the railroads changed from benevolence to hostility. Shippers demanded protection. And for this, they turned first to the legislatures of the states.[40]

One is tempted to say that the analogy between railroads at the turn of the last century and information technology companies at the start of the twenty-first century is almost exact. Both relied to some degree on public investments at their birth. The sheer transformative power of both technologies made them "affected with the public interest." The similar economic structures of the industries make steep price cutting in some markets, combined with the hope of charging above-cost prices in other markets or in later time periods, a prominent business strategy.

The debate over how or whether to regulate Microsoft and other information technology companies today stands pretty much where the debate over railroad regulation stood in the 1880s. Looking at what happened to the railroad industry after the 1880s provides insight into what could be the fate of the information technology industry if the same choices are made today.

Pressure to regulate railroads resulted in the passage in 1887 of the Act to Regulate Commerce, or as it would come to be known, the Interstate Commerce Act. The Act required that the rates charged by railroads be "reasonable" and "just," published in advance, and adhered to; that prior notice be given before rates were changed; that rebates no longer be given to favored shippers; and that other forms of price and service discrimination no longer be allowed.[41] The Interstate Commerce Commission—the first modern federal regulatory agency—was formed and given the task of enforcing the new Act.

Railroad lobbyists quickly complained it was unfair for railroads to be under ICC authority while their competitors—especially trucks and buses—were not. Trucking and bus companies largely agreed and supported amending the Interstate Commerce Act so they too would be safe from "ruinous competition." Soon after air travel became commercially viable, it was brought under similar control through the Civil Aeronautics Board. Prices were fixed and carriers were similarly protected from "too much" competition.

---

[40]Clair Wilcox, *Public Policies Toward Business, supra* note 34, page 369.

[41]*Ibid.*, page 371.

Through much of the twentieth century, the ICC was hailed as the epitome of scientific government. Clair Wilcox, author of the aforementioned textbook, once again expressed the consensus view of economists:

It is in the case of railroads that the federal government first undertook to regulate the operation of a private business. It is here that government has had its longest experience as a regulator and its greatest powers, that its regulatory activities have been most extensive, most intensive, and most detailed. It is here that regulation has been most effective and attended by the greatest measure of prestige.[42]

The ICC ruled over railroads, buses, and trucks for over a century, but the costs of regulatory intervention were much higher than originally thought.[43] Price-setting by bureaucracies was slow, inaccurate, and apt to be politicized, which tended to discourage innovation and efficiency. Interest groups both within and outside the railroad industry, such as unions, organized agriculture, and shippers, exploited the cartel-like arrangement to achieve special favors at the expense of the efficiency of the overall rail industry. Railroad unions, for example, negotiated high wages (relative to other, unregulated industries) for their members and work rules that lowered worker productivity (called "feather-bedding").[44]

At the same time, the benefits of ending "ruinous competition" turned out to be much smaller than the reformers had claimed.[45] The distinction between "ruinous" and "rigorous" competition, fuzzy in law as well as economic theory, turned out to be an artifact of interest group lobbying and not an objective fact. Scholarly research showed that the net effect of monopolies and collusion on

---

[42]*Ibid.*, page 368.

[43]For accounts of the unraveling of the public interest theory of antitrust, see Fred S. McChesney and William F. Shughart II, editors, *The Causes and Consequences of Antitrust, supra* note 17.

[44]Melvin Lurie, "The Effect of Unionization on Wages in the Transit Industry," *Journal of Political Economy* 69 (1961), pages 558-572.

[45]Richard A. Posner, *Natural Monopoly and Its Regulation* (Washington, DC: Cato Institute, 1999 [1969]), pages 47-51.

consumer prices,[46] company profits,[47] and the public's welfare[48] were very small (a tenth of one percent of the gross national product, in the case of public welfare) or even nonexistent.[49]

As the notion of "ruinous competition" was being discredited, regulations based on the notion wreaked havoc on the railroad industry. During the 1970s, between 20 percent (by rail mileage) and 33 percent (by rail revenue) of America's freight rail industry was in bankruptcy and the rate of return on investment was near zero.[50] The passenger rail industry's descent into bankruptcy occurred sooner. By 1919, 62 companies and 50 or more urban systems were in receivership and the industry was earning rates of return far below other industries.[51]

Responding to falling ridership and increasing costs, cities around the country made two fateful choices. First, they attempted to *erect barriers to entry* to the passenger rail industry so as to protect their local monopolists from less expensive and more convenient competitors. This was most clearly the case with regard to the use of personal cars or small vans to carry passengers, called "jitney" service. Laws forbidding the operation of jitneys appeared on the books almost as soon as cars started to appear in cities, and those restrictions remain on the books in nearly all major U.S. cities today.[52]

The second fateful decision by local elected officials was to *municipalize* local transit systems. By the mid-1960s, train and bus systems in most major U.S. cities were city-owned and heavily subsidized by tax revenues. County and state subsidies would soon follow; federal subsidies were first tapped in 1974. Revenue from fares fell from 82 percent of operating costs in 1970 to less than

---

[46]David Schwartzman, "The Effect of Monopoly on Price," *Journal of Political Economy* 67:4 (August 1959), pages 352-361.

[47]Peter Asch and Joseph J. Seneca, "Is Collusion Profitable?" in Fred S. McChesney and William F. Shughart II, editors, *The Causes and Consequences of Antitrust, supra* note 17, pages 107-117.

[48]Arnold C. Harberger, "Monopoly and Resource Allocation," *American Economic Review* 44:2 (May 1954), pages 77-87.

[49]Dominick T. Armentano, *Antitrust and Monopoly, supra* note 4, pages 20-34.

[50]Association of American Railroads, "H.R. 2784: Heavy Regulation and Bad Economics," position paper, n.d. (1999) http/www.aar.com.

[51]George W. Hilton, "The Rise and Fall of Monopolized Transit," in Charles A. Lave, editor, *Urban Transit: The Private Challenge to Public Transportation* (San Francisco, CA: Pacific Institute for Public Policy Research, 1985), page 39.

[52]*Ibid.*, pages 36-38. Other chapters in the same book explore jitney service and a variety of other private alternatives to public monopoly transit systems.

half in 1980.[53] In 1971, the nation's struggling inter-city passenger service lines were combined into Amtrak, and in 1976 seven bankrupt northeastern freight railroads were merged into Conrail. Rail service in the U.S. was widely recognized as expensive, inefficient, and, because of diminishing investment, increasingly unreliable.

Faced with either nationalizing the freight railroads or repealing counterproductive regulations, Congress chose the latter course and passed the Staggers Rail Act of 1980, which significantly scaled back regulations on railroads. In 1995 the ICC itself was abolished and a new agency, the Surface Transportation Board (STB), was created to oversee competition in the railroad industry. The STB retains a fairly narrowly defined authority to intervene in cases where it has proof that a railroad is using its control over its facilities to prevent a more efficient railroad from providing service to a "captive" customer.[54]

The results of deregulating the railroad industry have been dramatically positive. By 1998, rail shipping prices per ton-mile had fallen more than 50 percent in real terms, and average transit time and variations in transit time (a measure of delays) had both fallen at least 20 percent.[55] According to two industry experts writing in 1990,

> A rough calculation of annual total welfare gains in the United States from rail deregulation resulting from the Staggers Act would include something on the order of $5.3 to $7.2 billion in lower rates to shippers, $5 to $10 billion in reduced inventory-related logistics costs, slightly less than $500 million in higher profits to railroads, and slightly over $700 million in savings to taxpayers.[56]

Passenger rail service, which was nationalized rather than deregulated, has seen little if any improvement in recent years. Travel by mass transit continues to fall relative to travel by other means, and in 1992 accounted for just 1 percent

---

[53]*Ibid.*, page 48.

[54]Jerry Ellig, "Rails and Wires: What's the Difference?" *Capitol Comment* No. 225 (Washington, DC: Citizens for a Sound Economy, February 22, 1999), page 1.

[55]Clifford Winston, "U.S. Industry Adjustment to Economic Deregulation," *Journal of Economic Perspectives*, Summer 1998; see also Wesley W. Wilson and William W. Wilson, "Deregulation and Innovation in Railroad Shipping of Agricultural Commodities: 1972-1995," *Staff Paper Series*, North Dakota State University Department of Agricultural Economics, December 1998.

[56]Christopher C. Barnekov and A.N. Leit, "The Efficiency Effects of Railroad Deregulation in the United States," *International Journal of Transport Economics*, February 1990.

of total national surface travel and 2.3 percent of urban trips.[57] Federal subsidies to mass transit soared 1,600 percent between 1970 and 1980, a period when ridership increased just 18 percent.[58] Farebox receipts covered only 41 percent of operating costs in 1998, and only 29 percent of total spending, including capital spending, that year.[59] Proposals to build new transit lines have been few and far between, and when they are built they invariably carry a fraction of the number of riders originally forecast at costs that are often several times original estimates.

Automobiles

The regulatory history of trains can be contrasted with the history of automobiles, whose history as a mass consumer good started with the marketing of the Model T by Henry Ford in 1901. Ford lowered the price of a Model T from $825 in 1908 to $440 in 1914, and to just $345 in 1916.[60] The total number of cars sold rose from 11,000 in 1903 to 13 million in 1923 and 26.5 million in 1930.[61] In 1921, Ford had cornered over 60 percent of the automobile market and was earning returns of over 100 percent.

Fortunately for the American economy, President Warren Harding's administration took a relaxed attitude toward the Sherman Act. By the late 1930s, Ford had been overtaken by General Motors (which had been near bankruptcy in 1921) and by Chrysler Corporation (which did not exist in 1921).[62] Today the "big three" battle intensely for market share against each other as well as foreign manufacturers and their domestic operations.

Although periodic antitrust threats were made against the major automobile companies, few were ever pursued to a conviction. A 1941 case found General Motors guilty of violating the Sherman Act by requiring its dealers to finance

---

[57]James A. Dunn Jr., *Driving Forces: The Automobile, Its Enemies and the Politics of Mobility* (Washington, DC: Brookings Institution, 1998), pages 93ff.

[58]*Ibid.*, page 93.

[59]National Transit Database Summaries and Trends (http://www.ntdprogram.com), analysis provided to The Heartland Institute by Randal O'Toole.

[60]James D. Johnston, *Driving America: Your Car, Your Government, Your Choice* (Washington, DC: American Enterprise Institute, 1997), page 2.

[61]*Ibid.*, page 3.

[62]Yale Brozen, *Is the Government the Source of Monopoly?* (Washington, DC: Cato Institute, 1980), page 24.

installment sales of automobiles through GM Acceptance Corporation, a subsidiary, thereby excluding competitors from the car financing business.[63] In a 1966 case, General Motors and its dealers were told to stop actions aimed at preventing sales of Chevrolets through discounters.[64]

A popular myth concerning unfair competition between the makers of buses and petroleum, on the one hand, and mass transit systems on the other, arose from a report written by Bradford Snell for a U.S. Senate subcommittee in 1974.[65] According to Snell, major auto manufacturers were conspiring to put city mass transit operators out of business, and the "smoking gun" was a 1949 case called *U.S. v. National City Lines*, in which General Motors was charged with conspiring with Standard Oil of California and Firestone Tire and Rubber to buy up and then dismantle passenger train services in 45 cities, in order to replace them with GM buses rolling on Firestone tires and fueled by Standard Oil. All three companies were found guilty, and General Motors was charged $5,000.

Snell's account of this episode has been repeated so often it is almost a piece of American folklore. If true, it would lend credibility to allegations that major corporations, such as Microsoft, buy and then "sit on" or do not market innovative products created by their smaller competitors. But like other anecdotes that constitute much of the "evidence" put forward by antitrust's proponents, this story is apocryphal.

As James A. Dunn Jr., a professor of political science and public administration at Rutgers University-Camden,[66] explains, the *National City Lines* case focused on whether GM was attempting to corner the market on buses, not on unfair competition with mass transit companies. According to Cliff Slater, "GM did not cause the destruction of the streetcar systems. Streetcars are being replaced all over the world by buses on about the same time line as in the United States. GM simply took advantage of an economic trend . . . that was going to continue with or without GM's help."[67] Transportation economist George W. Hilton presented a detailed and devastating critique of Snell's theory in a statement included in the same publication as Snell's original

---

[63]*General Motors Corp. v. U.S.*, 121 F. 2nd 376, certiorari denied, 314 U.S. 618.

[64]*U.S. v. General Motors Corp.*, 384 U.S. 127.

[65]Bradford C. Snell, "American Ground Transportation: A Proposal for Restructuring the Automobile, Truck, Bus and Rail Industries," Appendix A, *Industrial Reorganization Act Hearings on S. 1167*, 93rd Congress, 1974.

[66]James A. Dunn Jr., *Driving Forces*, *supra* note 56, pages 7-10.

[67]Quoted in James A. Dunn Jr., *ibid.*, page 10.

charges appeared.[68]

The economic health and success of the automobile industry stands in striking contrast to that of the railroads, even after the partial recovery of the latter during the 1990s. For example, in 1996 there were 200 million cars and light trucks registered in the U.S., about two for every household. Though some people disdain the privately owned automobile,[69] there is no disputing the existence of a love affair between many Americans and their cars. As one automotive expert recently wrote,

> Getting into our cars is about like getting into our clothes—a daily necessity. Where we go, our cars go. Where our cars cannot go, most of us simply do not go. There are no possessions, other than our homes, upon which we Americans rely more than on our cars, vans, and trucks.[70]

The dominance of the automobile as the preferred form of American transportation probably is the result of many causes, some of them arising from the auto's convenience and privacy. Yet one should not underestimate the advantage enjoyed by American automobile manufacturers, who were driven by competition to respond quickly and efficiently to consumer demands, compared to the train and other common carrier industries, which spent most of the twentieth century in a regulated torpor.

It seems clear from this history that the information technology industry would do well to follow the example of the automobile industry and avoid close relationships with government, and especially avoid the distorting effects of antitrust regulation.

HISTORY OF THE MICROSOFT CASE

The passage of time allows us to compare predictions made at the beginning of

---

[68]George W. Hilton, "Statement of George W. Hilton, professor of economics, University of California at Los Angeles," *Industrial Reorganization Act Hearings on S.1167*, 93rd Congress, 1974. For more, see Cliff Slater, "General Motors and the Demise of Streetcars," 51 *Transportation Quarterly* 45-66 (1997).

[69]A criticism that is poorly supported, since switching from horses and mules to automobiles produced environmental benefits that exceeded the costs. See Joseph L. Bast and Jay Lehr, "The Increasing Sustainability of Cars, Trucks, and the Internal Combustion Engine," *Heartland Policy Study* No. 95 (Chicago, IL: The Heartland Institute, June 2000).

[70]James D. Johnston, *Driving America, supra* note 59, page 4.

the Microsoft case with actual events in the decade of Internet Time that has passed since the Microsoft case began. Microsoft's critics have been proven wrong at almost every turn.

In 1995, the Department of Justice entered into a consent decree with Microsoft regarding the marketing of Windows. Later, the government claimed the Decree barred Microsoft from integrating Internet Explorer into the Windows operating system. During 1997 and 1998, the government brought and lost a suit on this issue.

The government then brought a broad antitrust suit in May 1998. In June 2000, Judge Thomas Penfield Jackson granted the government's request for an order to have the company broken up, but then stayed the remedy pending the inevitable appeal. The Department of Justice asked the U.S. Supreme Court to hear the appeal, but on September 26, the Court ordered the Washington, D.C. Court of Appeals to review the case first. That is where the case stood at the time this book was written.

Dire Predictions

In the year before the introduction of Windows 95, Microsoft announced it would start its own online service, to be called Microsoft Network (MSN). An icon for MSN would appear on the Windows desktop. At the time of its announcement, Microsoft had a market share of exactly zero in the online services business. AOL promptly ran to the federal government to complain that Microsoft's plan was "anti-competitive." Steven Levy wrote an article in *Newsweek* warning that because of MSN, "One day, dollar bills may be replaced with Bill Dollars, and a piece of every online transaction could go through Microsoft's bulging coffers."[71]

Gary Reback, an attorney working for some of Microsoft's competitors, along with economists Brian Arthur and Garth Saloner (popularizers of the technological lock-in theory), explained "Why Microsoft Must Be Stopped":

> It is difficult to imagine that in an open society such as this one with multiple information sources, a single company could seize sufficient control of information transmission so as to constitute a threat to the underpinnings of free society. But such a scenario is a realistic (and

---

[71]Steven Levy, "Antitrust and Common Sense," *Newsweek*, March 6, 1995.

perhaps probable) outcome.[72]

Business Week worried Microsoft "can leverage" its operating system dominance to "corner" markets such as "networking, home software, and online services. In short, it might largely take control of the information superhighway."[73]

One newspaper's timeline of Microsoft's troubles with the DOJ stated that in May 1995, "Competitors complain to the department and the press that the bundling [of MSN with Windows 95] is anti-competitive and unfair."[74] "MSN could quickly dwarf other online services, some industry executives said," reported the *Wall Street Journal*.[75] The Antitrust Division was examining "whether Microsoft is illegally attempting to use its overwhelming dominance in operating systems to catapult into dominance of the online market."[76]

In 1997, the Council for a Competitive Electronic Marketplace warned that by using Windows, Microsoft would be able to capture customers for online services for products such as insurance, banking, real estate, and local entertainment. "No single entity or individual should control access to the electronic marketplace."[77]

Another group of Microsoft competitors (Netscape, Oracle, Sun, MCI) wanted government action so that Microsoft did not "gain control of the Internet" and urged that suppression of Microsoft was necessary to "ensure the accessibility and affordability of information technology and the Internet."[78]

Netscape's Jim Clark offered a similar warning: "[I]f Microsoft owns the browser as well as the operating system, there will be no Yahoo!, no Infoseek, no Excite, just Bill standing at the gate, pointing out where he wants to go.

---

[72]Gary L. Reback, Susan Creighton, David Killam, Neill Nathanson, Garth Saloner, and W. Brian Arthur, "Why Microsoft Must Be Stopped," *Upside Magazine*, February 1995, pages 52-67.

[73]"Sorry, Bill, the Deal is Off," *Business Week*, February 27, 1995, page 39.

[74]"The History of Microsoft vs. Uncle Sam," *Investor's Business Daily*, October 27, 1997.

[75]Viveca Novak and Don Clark, "Microsoft Corp. Broadly Attacks Antitrust Unit," *Wall Street Journal*, June 27, 1995.

[76]Viveca Novak and Don Clark, "U.S. Withdraws Subpoena to Microsoft," *Wall Street Journal*, July 24, 1995, page B5.

[77]"Going After Gates," *Business Week*, November 3, 1997, page 34.

[78]Adam Thierer, "Microsoft's Rivals Turn Left, Head for the Hill," *Investor's Business Daily*, September 12, 1997.

Microsoft will be the one and only 'portal'."[79]

Sun's Steve McNealy fretted: "How are you going to compete if Microsoft won't put you on the Microsoft Shopping Center—which will be the opening screen of everyone's computer?"[80]

In 1998, an advocacy group called ProComp warned of "the very real potential that Microsoft will become virtually the sole gateway to the digital marketplace."[81]

Ohio Attorney General Betty Montgomery warned that unless Microsoft was stopped, it would turn the "information superhighway" into a "toll road."[82] Sun praised the DOJ's lawsuit and intoned, "[N]o one company should gain a chokehold on the Internet."[83]

Similar warnings were made when Windows 98 made its debut with Channels (a soon-to-fail elaborate version of a "favorite links" list). "This, says the government, allows Microsoft to dominate entry to the Net and all electronic commerce."[84]

In 1998, the *New York Times* was still worried about MSN, reporting: "Competitors contend that the arrangement, called 'bundling,' would give Microsoft an unfair advantage in the new but fast-growing market for online services. The Justice Department's antitrust division is investigating those assertions."[85]

As late as April 2000, *after* AOL announced it would choose Netscape as the AOL browser, the Department of Justice was warning Judge Jackson that Microsoft might "add proprietary features to its Internet Explorer browser to tighten its control of the main on-ramp to the Internet for millions of consumers."[86] "Leveraging monopoly control of computer operating systems

---

[79]Jim Clark, *Netscape Time* (New York, NY: St. Martin's Press, 1999), page 243. After AOL bought Netscape, Clark used some of his profits to buy a million shares of Microsoft, and he now opposes the breakup plan. "Jim, Jim—Can't you afford to have some scruples?" asked *Inter@ctive Week*. "Crosstalk," *Inter@ctive Week*, July 31, 2000, page 102.

[80]Quoted in Richard B. McKenzie, *Trust on Trial*, *supra* note 4, page 205.

[81]"Why Consumers Should Care," www.procompetition.org/market/care.html.

[82]Quoted in Mark Schmidt, "Lawyers Playing Lawmakers: The Microsoft Antitrust Suit," National Taxpayers Union Foundation, 1999, page 3, www.ntu.org/issues/taxes/tech/pp119.htm.

[83]Sun press release dated May 19, 1998, quoted in Citizens Against Government Waste, "The Federal Assault on High Tech," February 9, 1999, page 11.

[84]"Settle the Microsoft Case," *Business Week*, June 1, 1998, page 170.

[85]Steve Lohr, "Citing Abuse, Microsoft Sues U.S. About its New Network," *New York Times*, June 27, 1998.

[86]John R. Wilke and Ted Bridis, "Enforcers Requested Microsoft Breakup as Best Solution to Thwart Monopoly," *Wall Street Journal*, May 1, 2000.

into monopoly control of the Net," said *Business Week* a month later, "is simply not acceptable."[87]

Failing the
Test of Time

Despite these warnings, nothing was done to stop Microsoft. While the pressure of the antitrust case may have forced Microsoft to stop enforcing some terms in contracts with some of its business partners, and may have distracted the company's leaders from producing new and better products, those setbacks were surely minor in light of Microsoft's supposedly immense market power.

Microsoft's sinister power has had two decades (Internet Time) to grow after Reback's warning and a decade (Internet Time) to grow since the DOJ filed suit against Microsoft. Yet the United States has not become the totalitarian nation forecast by Reback, Levy, and other Microsoft critics.

The Department of Justice, in a surprising fit of common sense, decided that preventing a company from competing in a new market would be difficult to justify on antitrust grounds. So Windows 95 made its debut with the MSN icon intact, and MSN went on to become the most expensive failure in Microsoft's history. MSN's content was weak, the interface was horrible, and the installation routine was lengthy and error-prone.

AOL, meanwhile, made its interface better and better, and marketed itself incessantly through free sign-up disks and by paying computer manufacturers to include an AOL icon on the Windows desktop screen. AOL has gobbled up Compuserve and now controls 25 million subscribers.[88] Microsoft Network, meanwhile, no longer exists as an online service. It has been replaced with a free Web portal, similar to the Yahoo! or Excite portals. Microsoft's Internet Service Provider business currently serves about 3 million customers.[89]

The fuss over Microsoft Network shows that antitrust was not needed even though MSN was on every desktop of every Windows 95 computer. MSN never came close to beating AOL because it was an inferior product. The MSN case also illustrates the power of technological change to eliminate incipient monopolies. The development of the Internet made online services much less

---

[87]"Microsoft: What to Do—and Not to Do," *Business Week*, April 20, 1998, page 170.

[88]Mindy Charski, "Microsoft Readies to Battle AOL for Browser Users," *Inter@ctive Week*, September 4, 2000, page 16.

[89]*Ibid.*

important than they used to be.

Allowing Microsoft to attempt to compete in the market for online services produced enormous benefits for consumers. When MSN was introduced, AOL was charging $54.20 for 20 hours of use a month. MSN was priced at $19.95 for that same amount of time.[90] Thanks in part to the competition created by MSN, AOL eventually dropped its price between $19.95 and $24.95 for *unlimited* use, and most other online services and Internet Service Providers followed suit.

The same story is repeated in virtually every area where Microsoft's entry was predicted to *reduce* competition and *harm* consumers.

After a brisk start, Microsoft has basically given up competing in the market for local entertainment guides. According to *Business Week*,

> Some 136 newspapers signed up with Zip2 Corp., a Mountain View (Calif.) supplier of online publishing technology that helps publishers create electronic versions of their newspapers. 'Microsoft tries to scare people into giving up, but it's just not working,' says Zip2 CEO Rich Sorkin, who claims that his combined newspaper sites are racking up 8 million viewers a month—nearly triple the traffic Microsoft's ten Sidewalk sites are drawing.[91]

Microsoft has since sold its Sidewalk sites. Microsoft's real estate site, HomeAdvisor, trails Homestore.com and is being forced, like many other e-commerce sites, to reconfigure its business strategy.[92]

On the other hand, Microsoft's online travel and automobile services are doing quite well, although they have captured much less than 50 percent of their markets.[93] It appears Microsoft's online services succeed when they please consumers and fail when they do not, which is what one would expect of a competitive marketplace.

---

[90]John Markoff, "U.S. Won't Challenge Microsoft Network Before Its Debut," *New York Times*, August 9, 1995, page C5.

[91]"Microsoft's Future," *Business Week*, January 19, 1998, page 68.

[92]Don Clark and Jerry Guidera, "Microsoft Plans to Unveil Home-Finance Venture," *Wall Street Journal*, March 16, 2000.

[93]*Ibid.*

Why the Predictions
Were False

One easy conclusion is that Microsoft's ownership of Windows and Internet Explorer is not enough to lead to control of online commerce. Microsoft competes with traditional bricks-and-mortar companies as well as their Web sites, other portals and online services with millions of users, and companies specializing in making e-commerce work. Even though Microsoft supplies the starting point for much Web surfing, "everything else is just a click away," explains an analyst with Forrester Research.[94]

More fundamentally, the idea that a Web browser could be used to control Internet content was hardly believable in the first place. One might as well believe that Sony would be able to control television programming if it sold 40 percent (or even 95 percent) of new television sets in the United States. A browser—like a television—is just a tool to reach content. A television or a browser that *interferes* with access to content is by definition an inferior product. It is not going to have a viable economic future, much less become a market leader.

The reason Microsoft has not tried to use its browser to start extracting Internet rents is the sheer impossibility of doing so. In 1997, Microsoft executive Nathan Myhrvold said the company wanted to get part of the "vig" (gambling slang for part of the transaction) for every Internet transaction using Microsoft software.[95] But Microsoft apparently realized that trying to use the browser to extract revenue from Web vendors or consumers would fail. Chris Hall and Robert Hall give this scenario for what would happen if Microsoft made the attempt:

> Yahoo! will ally with a manufacturer of cheap small computers and a national Internet service provider to produce an entire system that is Yahoo!-branded, defaults to the Yahoo! portal, but also provides access to the entire Internet with an open standard browser such as Netscape or Opera. The hardware would be cheap enough to be given away, like cellular phones or cable boxes, and all of the profit will be made from advertising, monthly fees, and transaction fees.[96]

---

[94]"Microsoft's Future," *Business Week, supra* note 90.

[95]John Heilemann, "The Truth, the Whole Truth and Nothing but the Truth," *supra* note 2, page 266.

[96]Chris E. Hall and Robert E. Hall, *National Policy on Microsoft: A Neutral Perspective* (version 2.0, 1999), pages 67-68, www.NetEcon.com.

Gates also hoped Microsoft could at least make money from banks whose customers used Microsoft Money personal finance software and the Microsoft Network to connect to a bank's computer system. But instead, banks simply created their own Web sites to serve their customers directly.

What about Web servers—the computers that serve up the Internet's content to Web surfers? Could a company leverage a huge market share for its browsers into control of the market for servers?

Netscape, during its period of early dominance, tried to do precisely this. Then Microsoft and other software developers came in and began underpricing Netscape. Today, the leading Web server software is Apache, a Unix-based program, which is free, and which is on 63 percent of servers. Microsoft's IIS is second, with 20 percent. Netscape's Enterprise has 7 percent.[97]

Even if Microsoft achieves a high share in the server operating system market, it is likely to have little market power, because barriers to entry are low. Server software, including the operating system, carries out a limited range of functions. The software provides only the simplest user interface, the source of much of the complexity in full operating systems.

What if Microsoft were the only browser company in the world? Could it then introduce a browser with Microsoft-only features and force the rest of the world to buy Microsoft server software, by making IE incompatible with every other company's Web server? An allegation to this effect was made in the spring of 2000 by the Department of Justice, although the court never heard evidence on the subject. It was alleged that Internet Explorer included proprietary extensions of Kereboros (a security program that prevents hackers from entering a Web site) that work best only with the Microsoft Web server.[98]

The first practical obstacle to this strategy is that users of Internet Explorer would be cut off from any Web site that did not fall in line with Microsoft's program. This would be a major competitive defect, to say the least. Older versions of Internet Explorer and any remaining copies of other browsers on the market would still be able to gain access to those sites. An immediate market would emerge for new browsers able to reach Web sites that did not adopt Microsoft's server software. Major Web sites, particularly portals, would give away such browsers to ensure their sites could be reached. AOL, as owner of Netscape, would be in a particularly good position if Microsoft altered Internet Explorer to make it incompatible with AOL and other Web sites.

Microsoft's hold on the browser market could never be strong enough to

---

[97]Netcraft Web Server Survey, June 2000, http://www.netcraft.com.

[98]John R. Wilke and Ted Bridis, "Enforcers Requested Microsoft Breakup as Best Solution to Thwart Monopoly," *supra* note 85.

allow it to extract significant value from the server side, despite Microsoft's important roles in providing both a browser and server software. Individual users would not have to play a major role in opposing Microsoft. Rather, key Web sites—valued in the stock market for tens of billions of dollars—would play that role.[99]

Because the Internet is so new and developing so rapidly, reporters and politicians are easy prey for manufactured panics. It would be much more difficult to create such a fright over a more familiar product, such as automobiles. Nobody would believe today that if General Motors opened its own chain of filling stations, the auto company would be on the verge of taking over all American transportation. But on the Internet, the theory seems to be that if you can't tell the male end of a dongle from a TCP stack, then you will be a sucker for silly claims about chokeholds.

Merely asserting that a company is a "monopolist" has allowed many of Microsoft's competitors to get a free ride from reporters and policymakers who ought to know better. For example, Jim Barksdale, then serving as the CEO of Netscape, told Congress in 1998:

> I was struck by the fact, in the response of Mr. Gates to the question about whether or not he was a monopoly, he talked about how short-lived the products were, and we all understand that. That doesn't negate whether or not it's a monopoly though. Even if it went away six months from now, it is a monopoly today.[100]

Such a claim cannot stand even casual scrutiny, yet it is characteristic of the terms of the debate in the Microsoft case. Those who use the tactic appear to suffer no loss in credibility. Steven Levy, the *Newsweek* writer who warned we'd all be using "Bill Dollars" by now, is still sharing his expertise with *Newsweek*'s readers. In June 2000 he penned a cover story advising Gates to capitulate to most of the government's demands.[101] Similarly, Sun's Scott McNealy applauded the Microsoft breakup order as a tool to "protect Internet technologies from becoming the proprietary presence of any one company."[102]

---

[99]Chris E. Hall and Robert E. Hall, *National Policy on Microsoft: A Neutral Perspective, supra* note 95, pages 73-74.

[100]"In Their Own Words: Three High-Tech CEOs Testify," *Wall Street Journal*, March 4, 1998.

[101]Steven Levy, "Know When to Fold 'Em, Bill," *Newsweek*, June 19, 2000, page 32.

[102]John Cook, "Microsoft's Competition Encouraged by Company's Distractions," *Seattle Post-Intelligencer*, June 8, 2000.

BRIEFLY STATED . . .

A close look at "antitrust's greatest hits"—the Standard Oil case of 1906, the Alcoa case in 1945, and the breakup of AT&T in 1981—reveals the same patterns of arbitrary rulings, disregard for consumers, and political interference with the administration of justice as are on display in the Microsoft case. Misinterpretations of these cases constitutes many of the "facts" and nearly all of the vocabulary used to defend antitrust law from its critics.

High-tech companies should look at the history of the transportation industry for insight into the choices they face. The railroad industry took the path of heavy-handed regulation, which created a legacy of inefficiency and bankruptcy that continues to the current day. In sharp contrast is the automobile industry, which was subject to relatively light regulation. Today that industry is characterized by innovation, growth, and responsiveness to consumers.

The much shorter history of the Microsoft case has exposed the exaggeration and falsehoods of Microsoft's critics. Where are Microsoft Network, Channels, and Sidewalk today? All have disappeared, become irrelevant, or been radically transformed due to superior competition and changing technology. The Internet remains free and decentralized, and for good reasons: Microsoft cannot "leverage" its dominance in a few markets into control over Internet access or content. To claim otherwise might sell news magazines or flummox Congressmen—but it is hardly telling the truth.

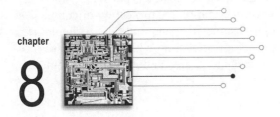

Antitrust
and Politics

     "T he central weakness of the antitrust literature has been
its reliance on presumptions," writes George Stigler.[1]
The presumptions that stand at the center of the case against Microsoft, and by
implication at the center of the case for applying antitrust law in the digital era,
are that antitrust laws were conceived as, and are currently enforced to be, a
reasonably effective solution to the problems of monopoly, collusion, and
concentration in industry. Those presumptions are eminently rebuttable.[2]

    The legislative record shows that the authors of the Sherman Act were
motivated by short-term political considerations, not a desire to protect the
public's welfare. Government officials charged with enforcing antitrust laws
have consistently targeted industries where prices are falling and output is
rising, just the opposite of what one would expect if their goal was consumer
protection. Finally, the Microsoft case itself provides ample evidence of
political interference in antitrust enforcement.

    The notion that antitrust and its enforcement are imbued with a love of the

---

[1]George Stigler, *The Organization of Industry* (Homewood, IL: Richard D. Irwin, Inc., 1968), page 260.

[2]Joseph Bast contributed to this chapter.

public good is much less plausible than the alternative, that antitrust is an inherently political device designed and used to advance particular interests. Those interests vary over time, but have in common the protection of companies that are slow to respond to changing consumer demand and new technologies. This theory of antitrust does a superior job of predicting when antitrust cases are brought forward and what their consequences are, and therefore should be preferred to the public interest theory.

THE ORIGINS OF ANTITRUST LAW

The Sherman Antitrust Act of 1890 can best be understood as a reaction against the Future Shock of its era. In the 1880s, the United States was changing rapidly—too rapidly, many people felt—from an agrarian to an industrial economy. Business owners both large and small saw in the rapidly changing technologies and new business models a threat to their current market shares and profit margins. They solicited protection from the federal government, and found it in antitrust legislation.

During the House debates on the Sherman Act, Representative William Mason complained, "Trusts have made products cheaper, have reduced prices." The benefit to consumers, he continued, "would not right the wrong done to the people of this country by the 'trusts' which have destroyed legitimate competition and driven honest men from legitimate business enterprises."[3]

Preventing monopolists from raising prices, it is true, was part of the original language of the Sherman Act when it was introduced, but as Dominick T. Armentano comments:

> However, this wording was ripped from the legislation as approved by the U.S. Senate; the Sherman Act as enacted into law does not mention the alleged "sole" purpose, that is, [preventing] the "enhancement of prices by combination." Moreover, at least through 1911, the legal enforcement of the Sherman Act had absolutely nothing to do with the substantive conduct and performance of the indicted corporations or, in other words, with whether there *had* been any "enhancement of prices" to the consumers.[4]

---

[3]Thomas J. DiLorenzo, "Antitrust," in *Cato Handbook for Congress: 105th Congress* (Washington, DC: Cato Institute, 1997), page 401.

[4]Dominick T. Armentano, *Antitrust and Monopoly: Anatomy of a Policy Failure* (Oakland, CA: Independent Institute: second edition, 1990), page 6.

This is a far cry from the "consumer protection" purpose that even antitrust critic Robert Bork was willing to concede in 1978.[5]

Is it true that the Sherman Act was passed to *keep prices high*, rather than to benefit consumers by preventing monopolists from "enhancing prices"? More evidence that this was the case can be found in the debate over antitrust taking place in the states around the time the Sherman Act was proposed and signed into law. Those debates are especially relevant because during that period of history, states nominated and elected their U.S. Senators, and the Sherman Act was proposed in the Senate.

In the years leading up to and immediately following the adoption of the Sherman Act, some 24 states passed antitrust legislation.[6] According to Thomas J. DiLorenzo, a major impetus behind these laws was falling prices paid to the producers of agricultural products, a phenomenon that producers blamed on centralized food and meat processors in Chicago. Output from the agricultural sector was rising rapidly and prices to consumers were falling, the result of advances in farming, transportation, and processing technologies. Beef tenderloins, for example, fell in price by nearly 38 percent between 1883 and 1889, and the price of pork fell more than 40 percent between 1880 and 1890.[7] The situation, in other words, was just the opposite of what one would expect to be the case if monopoly pricing were present.

If it was producer concern over *falling* agricultural prices rather than consumer concern over *rising* prices that fueled support for antitrust laws, then states that were most reliant on farming and cattle should have been more likely to adopt antitrust laws than other states. Were they? Two measures of states' reliance on agriculture—farms per capita and cows per capita—tested positive in a regression analysis performed by Boudreaux *et al.*, leading them to conclude, "the relative abundance in the economy of farms, and of cattle in particular, is an important predictor of which states passed antitrust laws after 1877."[8]

The Sherman Act, in short, was very likely passed to appease producer protests from the nation's heartland, and not to battle the scourge of anti-

---

[5]Robert Bork, *The Antitrust Paradox: A Policy at War with Itself* (New York, NY: Basic Books, 1978), page 66.

[6]The following discussion is based on Thomas J. DiLorenzo, "The Origins of Antitrust: An Interest-Group Perspective," *International Review of Law and Economics* 5 (1985), pages 73-90; and Donald J. Boudreaux, Thomas J. DiLorenzo, and Steven Parker, "Antitrust before the Sherman Act," in Fred S. McChesney and William F. Shughart II, editors, *The Causes and Consequences of Antitrust: The Public-Choice Perspective* (Chicago, IL: University of Chicago Press, 1995), pages 255-270.

[7]Donald J. Boudreaux, Thomas J. DiLorenzo, and Steven Parker, *ibid.*, page 259.

[8]*Ibid.*, page 270.

competitive practices by monopolists. Thomas Hazlett adds an interesting footnote to this discussion by making a persuasive case that the sponsors of the Sherman Act sought primarily to distract local voters from, and to trade votes in the House and Senate for, the McKinley Tariff, a pro-industry bill passed just six months later.[9] Either way, the oft-recited goals of efficiency, competition, and consumer benefits are at odds with the real history of antitrust law.

WINNERS AND LOSERS

If concern for the public interest determines when and how antitrust is used, then its history should reveal a pattern of use against industries that are concentrated, where monopoly profits are being earned, and where prices are rising—i.e., industries where anti-competitive acts may be causing some measurable welfare loss.

Economist George Stigler first raised the possibility that antitrust was not being used in the public interest in a pathbreaking study published in 1966.[10] Comparing rates of industry concentration from 1900 to 1960 for seven industries in the U.S. and in England (which at the time did not have antitrust laws), he concluded, "the Sherman Act appears to have had only a very modest effect in reducing concentration." He did, however, find a significant decrease in the number of horizontal mergers following passage in 1950 of an anti-merger statute.[11]

Law professor (and now federal judge) Richard A. Posner assembled a large database of U.S. antitrust cases filed between 1890 and 1969—a total of 1,551 cases—for an analysis first published in 1970.[12] While Posner again raised the possibility that politics, rather than the public good, may be guiding antitrust enforcement, he conducted only a rudimentary test of the hypothesis.[13] Three years later, however, a team of economists used Posner's database to conduct

---

[9]Thomas W. Hazlett, "The Legislative History of the Sherman Act Reexamined," *Economic Inquiry* 30 (1992), pages 263-276.

[10]George Stigler, "The Economic Effects of the Antitrust Laws," *Journal of Law and Economics* 9 (October 1966), reprinted in George Stigler, *The Organization of Industry, supra* note 1, pages 259-295.

[11]*Ibid.*, pages 270-271.

[12]Richard A. Posner, "A Statistical Study of Antitrust Enforcement," *Journal of Law and Economics* 13 (October 1970), pages 365-419.

[13]Posner looked for an association between the number of antitrust enforcement actions taken and which political party controlled the White House. There was no relationship.

a detailed statistical analysis of the probability of being targeted for antitrust action and an industry's sales, profits, concentration, and injury to consumers (welfare loss). They concluded:

> The empirical analysis suggests that industry size, as measured by sales, is the most important industry economic characteristic determining antitrust case-bringing activities. Variables more closely measuring monopoly actual or potential performance, such as profit rate on sales, concentration, and aggregate welfare losses play a less important role in explaining antitrust activity.[14]

The authors found "no statistically significant relationship between concentration and cases brought. . . ."[15] Later researchers have concurred.[16]

Research conducted by Charlie Weir, first published in 1992, found little evidence that antitrust laws in England are used to advance the public interest.[17] The government commission charged with challenging mergers that might be "against the public interest" placed little or no weight on such obvious matters of public interest as "price reductions, increased efficiency, improving the balance of payments, better management, more employment, and better research and development."[18] Nor were the relative profitability or market shares of the merger candidates significant factors.

Empirical analysis by Thomas DiLorenzo has found that all of the industries targeted by antitrust prosecutors in the U.S. were experiencing *rising* output and *falling* prices in the decade before enactment of the Sherman Act.[19] This is either evidence that the officials implementing the Sherman Act are grossly incompetent at finding real monopolists, or that they are pursuing some agenda different from what the general public believes.

---

[14]William Long, Richard Schramm, and Robert Tollison, "The Economic Determinants of Antitrust Activity," *Journal of Law and Economics* 16 (October 1973), reprinted in Fred S. McChesney and William F. Shughart II, editors, *The Causes and Consequences of Antitrust, supra* note 6, pages 95-105.

[15]*Ibid.*, page 102.

[16]See sources cited in Fred S. McChesney and William F. Shughart II, editors, *The Causes and Consequences of Antitrust, supra* note 6, page 30.

[17]Charlie Weir, "Monopolies and Mergers Commission, Merger Reports and the Public Interest: Probit Analysis," *Applied Economics* 24 (January 1992), pages 27-34, reprinted in Fred S. McChesney and William F. Shughart II, editors, *The Causes and Consequences of Antitrust, supra* note 6, page 235.

[18]*Ibid.*, page 237.

[19]Thomas J. DiLorenzo, "The Origins of Antitrust: An Interest-Group Perspective," *supra* note 6, pages 73-90.

PORK-BARREL JUSTICE

Northwest Airlines was told it might be the target of an antitrust case if it started flying passengers from Nevada to the West Coast. The threat came from then-Transportation Secretary Federico Peña, acting at the behest of Nevada's two senators, who in turn may have been acting at the behest of Reno Air, a Nevada airline that stood to lose revenue if it faced competition on these routes.

Of course, it may only be a coincidence that the two senators chose to defend a firm that happens to be located in the state they represent in Washington. More likely, though, Reno Air communicates regularly with its senators, and took the opportunity to explain how it would be in everyone's best interest (that is, in the airline's and the senators' best interests) if Northwest Air were dissuaded from competing for customers in Nevada.

The Reno Air case is an example of how politics chooses the targets of antitrust cases. The U.S. Senate in 1890 approved the Sherman Act because rural agricultural interests pressed their elected representatives in Washington to protect them from falling prices and growing competition from larger competitors. The U.S. Senate today could change the wording of the Act to ensure it targets only firms that are raising prices and reducing output, but it chooses not to. Why?

The hundred-year record of antitrust law enforcement suggests Congress *wants* laws that are vague so members of Congress can help constituents by either targeting their competitors for prosecution or defending them when targeted by others. Congress *wants* a law that can be used to protect small businesses from larger competitors because there are more of the former than of the latter, and the latter are less likely to be present in every Congressional district.[20]

The bureaucrats who staff the Department of Justice and the Federal Trade Commission have their own agendas as well. They are not paid according to whether they target real monopolists, or by the social welfare loss they help society avoid, or according to any other measure related to the public interest. They are paid according to their ability to respond quickly and effectively to instructions from congressional committees that oversee their activities and therefore their budgets.

Does this sound too harsh? It shouldn't. In a remarkable piece of investigative research first published in 1987, Roger Faith, Donald Leavens, and Robert Tollison studied whether congressmen who hold positions on

---

[20]Bruce M. Benson, M.L. Greenhut, and Randall G. Holcombe, "Interest Groups and the Antitrust Paradox," *Cato Journal* 6 (Winter 1987), pages 801-818; William Baumol and Janusz Ordover, "Use of Antitrust to Subvert Competition," *Journal of Law & Economics* 28 (May 1985), pages 247-265.

committees that oversee the Federal Trade Commission or that control its budget use their authority to dismiss complaints and cases brought against firms in their districts and to sue competitors in other districts.[21] The researchers found much higher ratios of dismissals to complaints and of dismissals to cases brought against firms located in districts represented by members of two senate committees and three house committees with authority over the FTC's budget during the 1960s, and even more pronounced influence during the 1970s (following a reorganization of the FTC supposedly intended to *reduce* political interference). According to the authors, these results

> tend to bear out the pork-barrel hypothesis for both definitions of FTC activity. This is probably the strongest counter evidence to the claim that the reforms of the FTC altered the basic underlying relationship of the agency with Congress. If anything, the pork-barrel process became more pronounced and apparent in the data.[22]

Few defenders of antitrust law in general, or the case against Microsoft in particular, seem to realize how politicized the administration of the laws is in practice. Economic analysis, consumer interests, and the public interest all seem far removed from the day-to-day operation of the FTC and DOJ.

POLITICS AND THE MICROSOFT CASE

The Federal Trade Commission (in the early 1990s) and the Department of Justice (since 1993) did not develop an interest in Microsoft by reading computer industry news magazines. To the contrary, they began to notice Microsoft only after a persistent and well-financed lobbying campaign by various Microsoft competitors.[23]

---

[21]Roger L. Faith, Donald R. Leavens, and Robert D. Tollison, "Antitrust Pork Barrel," *Journal of Law and Economics* 25 (October 1982), pages 329-342, reprinted in Fred S. McChesney and William F. Shughart II, editors, *The Causes and Consequences of Antitrust, supra* note 6, pages 201-212.

[22]*Ibid.*, page 210.

[23]John Heilemann, "The Truth, the Whole Truth and Nothing but the Truth," *Wired*, November 2000, page 264.

Lobbying
by NOISE

The acronym for the loose alliance of Microsoft competitors is NOISE (Netscape, Oracle,[24] IBM, Sun, Everyone else). Among the most prominent companies in "everyone else" is Novell, a Utah-based company that has suffered doubly at the hands of Microsoft. Novell's small-office networking business has been eroded by the networking capabilities built into Windows 95 and improved in Windows 98. Novell also bought WordPerfect when it was still the leading word processor, then sold it a few years later at a loss of hundreds of millions dollars, as WordPerfect was supplanted by Word.[25]

Utah is also the home state of Senator Orrin Hatch, chair of the Senate Judiciary Committee. His widely publicized anti-Microsoft hearings helped lay the political foundation for the DOJ antitrust prosecution.

As noted earlier, AOL was also an important member of NOISE, even before it acquired Netscape. While Netscape sincerely cared about Internet Explorer—as a threat to Jim Barksdale's "God-given right to a 90 percent market share"—the rest of the NOISE coalition probably did not.

The core of NOISE is the "OIS" companies—Oracle, IBM, and Sun. Oracle and Sun sell almost exclusively to businesses, while IBM sells to businesses and consumers. For all three companies, the model has usually been strong product integration, high price, and low volume.

Sun does not merely integrate a Web browser into its Sun Solaris operating system: If you want to buy the Sun operating system, you must buy Sun microprocessors, storage, system software, and middleware. If you want a Sun Server, you must buy Sun workstations, the Sun Solaris operating system (a version of Unix), and Sun software. The same non-choice is offered to business network customers of IBM. Likewise, Oracle requires customers who want to buy Oracle servers to buy Oracle software.

The Microsoft breakup would be a huge benefit to Sun, which sells a Sun database program integrated with the Sun operating system. The separation of Microsoft Windows from the Microsoft application company would prevent Microsoft from competing effectively with Sun in the high-end corporate market. Should the Windows company attempt to create a new database

---

[24]Oracle hired a "detective" agency to steal trash from organizations that spoke out in favor of Microsoft. Associated Press, "Oracle Hired Detectives to Investigate Microsoft's Allies," *Seattle Post-Intelligencer*, June 28, 2000. The Heartland Institute (Chicago, Illinois) and the Independence Institute (Golden, Colorado) were not among the targets. The Independent Institute (Oakland, California) was.

[25]See Chapter 3 of this book for a discussion of how poor management, especially during the Novell years, threw away WordPerfect's leading position.

program, Sun could tie up the new product in court by calling it illegal middleware. (If the Office applications suite is "middleware," so is a database application.)

No one challenged the OIS model of making customers buy everything from a single source until Microsoft entered the market in the early 1990s. Microsoft's Windows NT operating system for servers is not bundled with Microsoft hardware and works on many different kinds of computers. The NT software is also simpler to use, has a well-designed and user-friendly graphical interface, and is cheaper than the products from the established companies. Computer hardware to run Windows NT machines is made by many different companies and is significantly cheaper than the proprietary Unix machines made by Sun.[26] With Windows NT as a platform, low-cost hardware companies like Dell and Gateway (which at the time knew a lot about Windows, but nothing about Unix) could start taking sales away from the OIS companies' more expensive machines.[27]

Microsoft Windows 3.1, and then Windows 95 and Windows 98 (for the desktop market, not the server market) were cash cows that gave Microsoft the resources to get into the server software business. Moreover, their popular graphical interface made many office workers eager for their companies to adopt Windows NT—since the worker could use an interface like the one already familiar from her home computer.

The three OIS companies suddenly became quite expert in discerning antitrust violations by their new competitor. Was Microsoft's style of competition really different from that of the NOISE companies? As detailed earlier, every weapon Microsoft used in the browser war was also used by Netscape, which started the war with a 90 percent monopoly-level share.

One IT company CEO who doesn't think Microsoft's conduct differed at all from that of its competitors is Doug Colbeth, creator of the Spyglass browser, which Microsoft bought and turned into Internet Explorer. When Microsoft started giving the browser away for free, Colbeth's licensing agreement became worthless, making him an unlikely ally of Microsoft. But in a 1999 interview, Colbeth said, "I think the government should stay out of it." He continued, "Barksdale, McNealy, they've all done what Gates has done." In fact, Colbeth said, "There is nothing there that I wouldn't have done."[28]

---

[26]"Operation Sunblock: Microsoft Goes to War," *Business Week*, October 27, 1997, page 114.

[27]Richard B. McKenzie, *Trust on Trial: How the Microsoft Case is Reframing the Rules of Competition* (Cambridge, MA: Perseus Books, 2000), page 126.

[28]Andrew Zajac, "It's Wait, Debate on Microsoft," *Chicago Tribune*, September 26, 1999, page 1.

Spyglass, incidentally, is doing just fine these days, notwithstanding Microsoft having devastated its former key product. The company responded by developing software for non-PC Internet connections—and won contracts from Xerox for Web-enabled photocopiers and from Motorola for an Internet appliance. In March 2000, Spyglass was purchased by OpenTV (a California company), so that Spyglass could develop software platforms for Internet television and wireless phones.[29]

Cisco Systems

If there is any company in the world that may have a "chokehold on the Internet," it is Cisco Systems, which makes 89 percent of high-end routers.[30] The *Wall Street Journal* summarizes Cisco's situation:

Cisco has eclipsed Microsoft in market capitalization; it dominates its marketplace, for computer networking equipment, in much the same way that Microsoft dominates PC operating systems and applications. Cisco also has a proprietary software product—its IOS operating system—that makes it hard for customers to switch to other suppliers.[31]

It boasts a 62 percent market share for its core product. It aggressively acquires emerging technologies and grafts them onto its flagship products. And its market power is so great that three of its most entrenched rivals have surrendered in the past year.[32]

Cisco's nearest competitor has a mere 5 percent market share.[33] But Cisco has remained unnoticed as a "monopoly" by the Department of Justice and by senators of both parties. It may be sheer coincidence, or it may be because Cisco was one of the first computer companies to start donating large amounts of hard

---

[29]Jon Van, "OpenTV, Spyglass of Naperville to Merge Operations," *Chicago Tribune*, March 27, 2000; Howard Wolinsky, "Net TV Firm to Buy Local Web Pioneer," *Chicago Sun-Times*, March 28, 2000, page 45.

[30]Ben Domenech, "Nader Sells Out," *National Review Online*, June 26, 2000, www.nationalreview.com.

[31]"After the Verdict, Companies Consider the Impact," *Wall Street Journal*, April 4, 2000, page A16.

[32]Scott Thurm, "Microsoft's Behavior is Helping Cisco Learn How to Avoid Trouble," *Wall Street Journal*, June 1, 2000.

[33]*Ibid.*

and soft money to both political parties.[34] Cisco decided early "to invest resources in Washington," and Cisco's lobbyists are careful to avoid taking a confrontational stance toward regulators.[35]

So in the funny world of antitrust, one company makes hardware (a router) costing thousands of dollars; the company captures most of the market, and even runs advertisements bragging that every Internet transaction in the world passes through its equipment. The second company makes software (a browser) it gives away for free, never captures more than 62 percent of its market, and (in 2001) ends up in second place. Which company gets prosecuted by the government for allegedly trying to establish a "chokehold on the Internet?"

This should not be construed as a call for antitrust prosecution of Cisco, which by all accounts has earned its near-monopoly status by producing superior products at costs lower than its competitors. Moreover, it should be noted that Cisco's electronics routers are on the verge of being made obsolete by the deployment of photonics routers, still another case of technological change making monopolies a matter of only fleeting concern in the digital era.[36] Still, it is difficult to understand why, if politics do not play a role in the selection of targets for antitrust prosecution, Microsoft rather than Cisco stands convicted of being too big and too successful.

Microsoft's Lobbying

Something else has happened—at near Internet speed—since the DOJ began harassing Microsoft. Formerly a company proud to stay out of politics,[37] Microsoft has bought itself a major lobbying presence in Washington and is donating huge sums of soft money to the two major parties and hard money to various candidates.

Microsoft's financial and lobbying involvement in Washington was puny even after an FTC investigation in the early 1990s, a Department of Justice investigation culminating in the 1995 consent decree, and a 1997-1998 lawsuit over the consent decree (in which Microsoft's interpretation was vindicated). In 1994, the company had one lobbyist in Washington; in 1997, it had only three,

---

[34]Greg Hitt, "Cisco's Chambers Revs Up Political Contribution Engine," *Wall Street Journal*, June 8, 2000.

[35]Scott Thurm, "Microsoft's Behavior is Helping Cisco Learn How to Avoid Trouble," *supra* note 32.

[36]George Gilder, "A Death Foretold," *Forbes ASAP*, February 21, 2000, page 145.

[37]Rajiv Chandraskekaran, "Microsoft's Window of Influence," *Washington Post*, May 7, 1999, page A1.

although by 1997 the company also had contracts with professional lobbyists.[38] In late 1997, Microsoft "had zero presence on the Hill," according to Rep. David McIntosh (R-Indiana).[39]

The May 1998 antitrust lawsuit finally pushed Microsoft into the ranks of companies under political attack that must spend as much money as necessary on lobbying and campaign contributions to protect themselves. Its PAC, which spent only $16,000 in 1995 (on copyright and encryption issues), now ranks as the third-largest corporate donor in the U.S.[40]

Microsoft's belated self-defense spurred Microsoft's competitors, who got into the influence-buying game years earlier, to complain that Microsoft was trying to buy justice. Their *paid consultant*, Robert Bork, fretted, "There is so much Microsoft money flowing through the system that the danger for nonpoliticized law is very real."[41]

This is like Hirohito complaining that American submarines were threatening to militarize the Pacific Ocean. If the Department of Justice and its Antitrust Division were not already politicized, there would never have been a Microsoft case. In 1999, Microsoft spent $4.6 million on lobbying, compared to $11 million by anti-Microsoft companies.[42]

Microsoft's competitors were similarly moved to complain when Microsoft and its allies lobbied against a record budget increase for the Department of Justice's Antitrust Division. But this could hardly be inappropriate conduct on Microsoft's part, any more than it would be wrong for the victims of abusive enforcement tactics by the Internal Revenue Service to lobby against a higher IRS budget. Microsoft's only mistake was that it didn't start lobbying *much sooner* to reduce the budgets (or even to eliminate the budgets) of the abusive divisions and bureaus housed in the Department of Injustice. When a pack of wolves is tearing into one's tent, an interest in predator control is legitimate, even if belated.

---

[38]Lizette Alvarez, "Stung by a Government It Ignored, Microsoft Abandons Isolationism," *New York Times*, December 21, 1997.

[39]John J. Miller, "Program Upgrade," *National Review*, February 8, 1999, page 33.

[40]Richard B. McKenzie, *Trust on Trial*, *supra* note 26, page 168.

[41]Robert H. Bork, "There's No Choice: Dismember Microsoft," *Wall Street Journal*, May 1, 2000.

[42]John Broder, "Microsoft Seeks Support through Huge PR Effort," *New York Times*, June 12, 2000.

BRIEFLY STATED . . .

Antitrust enforcement today is often accompanied by pro-consumer rhetoric, but the reality is that the Sherman Act began as a tool for politicians to protect constituents threatened by more successful business competitors. Sherman Act enforcement may temporarily decline, as it did under the Reagan and Bush administrations, but as long as the Act is on the books, it is a handy tool for abuse and extortion of American business.

A remarkable body of literature has been produced by economists and legal historians documenting the uses and consequences of antitrust laws. Much more plausible than the "public interest" theory of antitrust—that it exists to protect consumers from monopolists who would raise prices and reduce supply—is the "pork barrel" theory of antitrust—that it exists to give members of Congress the power to help or punish a constituent, without regard to the legality or social consequences of the targeted companies' business practices.

The case against Microsoft was driven by the political lobbying of its competitors, and it was to be expected that Microsoft would eventually respond by investing in politics itself. But as any reader without an axe to grind in this matter should readily agree, it is a shame that a company as innovative and valuable as Microsoft should be forced to devote resources to defending itself in the political arena from competitors who cannot compete successfully in the marketplace.

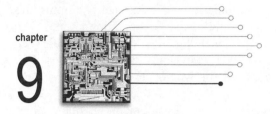

Conclusion

I t is easy to see how antitrust, properly used, could benefit consumers by deterring conspiracies to raise prices and reduce output. Yet the Microsoft case is a vivid example of why antitrust laws, as written and used today, injure rather than benefit consumers.

Milton Friedman, the Nobel Prize-winning economist, was long a critic of the practice of antitrust but not the theory. More recently he's changed his mind:

> [A]s I watched what actually happened, I saw that, instead of promoting competition, antitrust laws tended to do exactly the opposite, because they tended, like so many governmental activities, to be taken over by people they were supposed to regulate and control. And so, over time, I have gradually come to the conclusion that antitrust laws do far more harm than good, and that we would be better off if we didn't have them at all, if we could get rid of them.[1]

---

[1]Milton Friedman, "The Risky Road to Regulation," *National Post*, July 5, 1999, page C6, quoted in Richard B. McKenzie, *Trust on Trial: How the Microsoft Case is Reframing the Rules of Competition* (Cambridge, MA: Perseus Books, 2000), page 152.

Since the Microsoft case began a decade ago in Internet Time, Microsoft has faced two major new competitors in the operating systems market: Linux and a resurgent Apple. The exploding popularity of the Internet is diminishing the importance of the personal computer and of the PC operating system. The hottest new items in computing are personal digital assistants, digital Web phones, Internet appliances, Web-enabled television, game machines that compute, and other non-PC devices where Microsoft's advantage in PC operating systems counts for little.

Vastly increased bandwidth, thanks to new developments in fiber optics, will continue to make the Internet more important and the PC less so. As the information explosion created by the Internet drives out inefficiencies and drives down prices, the prospect of any company reaping monopoly profits in the digital era looks more and more remote.

Meanwhile Netscape, the official victim of the Microsoft case, has merged with AOL to create a company with far more "eyeball power" on the Web and far more paying Internet customers than Microsoft ever had. The "chokehold on the Internet" never developed, the First Amendment remains intact, and none of the other warnings about Microsoft came to pass.

Whatever economic relevance the Sherman Act had to an economy that was primarily farming and secondarily heavy manufacturing, it has none in the digital era. That is why the anti-Microsoft case became obsolete even before the trial ended in 2000 and the appeals began.

The present study has not attempted to survey every issue related to the Sherman Act. There has been no discussion of private antitrust lawsuits, which research suggests are nearly always illegitimate attempts by companies to suppress competition.[2] Nor has this study looked in detail at the Sherman Act's use to block mergers and acquisitions. There is considerable evidence suggesting that the Sherman Act's role in this regard is no more constructive than its role in government-brought prosecutions under Section One or Section Two.[3]

This study has dealt in only a passing manner with the Clayton Act and the Federal Trade Commission. Professor Dominick T. Armentano's excellent book, *Antitrust and Monopoly: Anatomy of a Policy Failure*, cited frequently in previous chapters, offers a comprehensive analysis of these and other antitrust

---

[2]Fred L. Smith Jr., "Why Not Abolish Antitrust?" *Regulation*, January/February 1983, page 28. According to Smith, "from July 1976 to July 1977, private parties filed 1,600 antitrust suits in federal courts, while government filed only 78."

[3]See, for example, Robert B. Ekelund Jr., Ph.D. and Mark Thornton, Ph.D., "The Cost of Merger Delay in Restructuring Industries," *Heartland Policy Study* No. 90 (Chicago, IL: The Heartland Institute, June 23, 1999).

laws and enforcement agencies and shows why *none* of them protects consumers.

Even if there were such a thing as a pro-consumer antitrust rule, it would have little relevance in Internet Time. Jim Barksdale's testimony to Congress, quoted in the previous chapter, suggested the duration of a monopoly is irrelevant to the question of what should be done to maintain competition in the information technology marketplace. But if the "monopoly" is likely to have a shorter lifespan than the time it takes to try an antitrust case, then the rationale for government action is considerably weaker; indeed, it disappears entirely.

Paradoxically, the very speed of technological intervention in the digital era, while making antitrust obsolete, increases the opportunities for predatory government intervention. When the automobile was invented, for example, the Supreme Court authorized warrantless searches of automobiles that never would have been tolerated for travelers on horseback.[4] The more novel the product is, the fewer companies there are with a stake in the right to introduce it, the fewer customers with a stake in the right to use it, and therefore the less resistance is mounted to government intervention.

It is true, then, that the Sherman Act is particularly harmful and unnecessary in the digital era. But this is like saying eating arsenic is particularly harmful and unnecessary in our nutrition-conscious society. The Sherman Act's flaws are as old as the battle for freedom against arbitrary and unjust government power. In the year 1215, England's King John was forced to swear in the Magna Carta that no one would be deprived of liberty or property except according to "the law of the land." The Sherman Act forbids ordinary conduct retroactively, and is so unbounded that businesses cannot know what is or is not "the law of the land."

The history of 110 years of Sherman Act prosecutions shows that waiting for principled, consistent, pro-competitive enforcement of the Act is like waiting for Godot. It theoretically could come, but there is little reason to believe it ever will; even if it did, there is no reason to believe it would stay for long.

Joel Klein, the head of the DOJ Antitrust Division who launched the case against Microsoft, resigned in September 2000, following the Supreme Court's refusal to bypass the District Court of Appeals and hear Microsoft's appeal immediately. The Associated Press summarized Klein's career as follows:

During Klein's tenure, which began October 18, 1996, the government blocked or altered about 170 mergers. In 220 criminal price-fixing cases, 52 executives were sent to prison, corporations paid $1.7 billion

---

[4]*Carroll v. United States*, 267 U.S. 132 (1925).

in fines and individuals paid another $21 million.[5]

In June 2000, Klein told an audience, "While technology changes, human nature does not. . . . When it comes to antitrust enforcement, the new, new thing isn't so new after all."[6]

Mr. Klein is exactly right. There is nothing we can do to prevent some people from fearing rapid change. But we *can* reduce the risk that fear-mongering will cause the government to harm innocents. Open-ended laws allowing unpopular people and industries to be prosecuted on vague and shifting grounds are an invitation to abuse, especially during periods of destabilizing change. Anti-trust statutes, like anti-witchcraft statutes, are archaic relics of fear. Neither has a place in the digital era.

The original draft of the Sherman Act outlawed only business arrangements that "advance the cost to the consumer." To amend the Sherman Act to restore this original language would be an improvement. Seriously applied, the language would prevent the prosecution of every antitrust case mentioned in this study, including the prosecution of Microsoft for giving software away for free.

But given the creative sophistry of the Antitrust Division, and the willingness of much of the federal judiciary to do the bidding of individual members of Congress, it may be unrealistic to expect that even restoring the original explicit language of the Sherman Act would narrow the Act's enforcement to cases of genuine consumer harm. After all, Internet Explorer wasted 17 cents' worth of hard disk space owned by consumers who did not want to browse the Internet.

The Microsoft case is not an isolated example of prosecutorial excess. It is the flagship case of antitrust at the beginning of the twenty-first century. The Antitrust Division loudly promises the Microsoft case is the vanguard of many more information technology cases to come. If the Microsoft case is the best the Antitrust Division has to offer America, then there is nothing of value in the Sherman Act. It is time to repeal that remnant of a less enlightened and much slower-paced era.

---

[5]Associated Press, "Antitrust Head Klein Leaving Government," September 19, 2000.

[6]"Microsoft Shakes Up Economic Models," *Wall Street Journal*, June 9, 2000, page A8.

Selected
Bibliography

Armentano, Dominick T. 1999. *Antitrust: The Case for Repeal*. Auburn, AL: Ludwig Von Mises Institute, second edition.

_____. 1990. *Antitrust and Monopoly: Anatomy of a Policy Failure*. Oakland, CA: Independent Institute, second edition.

_____. ____. *The Myths of Antitrust*. New York, NY: Arlington House.

Arthur, W. Brian. 1994. *Increasing Returns and Path Dependence in the Economy*. Ann Arbor, MI: University of Michigan Press.

Barfield, Claude E. and William A. Schambra, editors, 1986. *The Politics of Industrial Policy*. Washington, DC: American Enterprise Institute.

Bork, Robert H. 1978. *The Antitrust Paradox: A Policy at War with Itself*. New York, NY: Basic Books.

Bradley, Robert L. Jr. 1996. *Oil, Gas, and Government: The U.S. Experience*. Washington, DC: Cato Institute.

Brozen, Yale. 1980. *Is the Government the Source of Monopoly?* Washington, DC: Cato Institute.

Buchanan, James M. 1987 [1967]. *Public Finance in Democratic Process.* Chapel Hill, NC: The University of North Carolina Press.

Christensen, Clayton M. 1997. *The Innovator's Dilemma: When New Technologies Cause Great Firms to Fail.* Boston, MA: Harvard Business School Press.

Clark, J. Stanley. 1958. *The Oil Century.* Norman, OK: University of Oklahoma Press.

Crandall, Robert and Jerry Ellig. 1997. *Economic Deregulation and Consumer Choice: Lessons for the Electric Industry.* Fairfax, VA: Center for Market Processes.

DiLorenzo, Thomas J. 1997. "Antitrust," in *Cato Handbook for Congress: 105th Congress.* Washington, DC: Cato Institute.

Dorn, James A., editor. 1984. "Planning America: Government or the Market?" *The Cato Journal.* Volume 4, Number 2 (Fall).

Dunn, James A. Jr. 1998. *Driving Forces: The Automobile, Its Enemies and the Politics of Mobility.* Washington, DC: Brookings Institution.

Epstein, Richard. 1998. *Principles for a Free Society: Reconciling Individual Liberty with the Common Good.* Reading, MA: Perseus Books.

Evans, David S., Franklin M. Fisher, Daniel L. Rubinfeld, and Richard L. Schmalensee. 2000. *Did Microsoft Harm Consumers? Two Opposing Views.* Washington, DC: AEI-Brookings Joint Center for Regulatory Studies.

Evans, Philip and Thomas S. Wurster. 2000. *Blown to Bits: How the New Economics of Information Transforms Strategy.* Boston, MA: Harvard Business School Press.

Fagin, Barry. 1999. *The Case Against the Case Against Microsoft.* Washington, DC: Competitive Enterprise Institute.

Folsom, Burton W. 1993 (3d edition). *The Myth of the Robber Barons.* Herndon, VA: Young America's Foundation.

Furnas, J.C. 1969. *The Americans: A Social History of the United States, 1587-1914.* New York, NY: G.P. Putnam's Sons.

Gates, Bill. 1999. *Business @ the Speed of Thought: Using a Digital Nervous System.* New York, NY: Warner Books.

Hall, Chris E. and Robert E. Hall. 1999. *National Policy on Microsoft: A Neutral Perspective.* Version 2.0 (February 27, 1999). www.NetEcon.com.

Hilton, George W. 1974. "Statement of George W. Hilton, professor of economics, University of California at Los Angeles," in *Industrial Reorganization Act Hearings on S.1167*, 93rd Congress.

Huber, Peter W. *Orwell's Revenge: The 1984 Palimpsest.* 1994. New York, NY: Free Press.

Huber, Peter W., Michael K. Kellogg, and John Thorne. 1999. *Federal Telecommunications Law.* Laithersburg, NY: Aspen Publishing.

Johnston, James D. 1997. *Driving America: Your Car, Your Government, Your Choice.* Washington, DC: American Enterprise Institute.

Jones, Howard Mumford. 1971. *The Age of Energy: Varieties of American Experience, 1865-1915.* New York, NY: The Viking Press.

Josephson, Matthew. 1934. *The Robber Barons: The Great American Capitalists, 1861-1901.* New York, NY: Harcourt, Brace and Company.

Lave, Charles A., editor. 1985. *Urban Transit: The Private Challenge to Public Transportation.* San Francisco, CA: Pacific Institute for Public Policy Research.

Levy, Robert A. 1999. "Microsoft Redux: Anatomy of a Baseless Lawsuit." *Policy Analysis* No. 352. Washington, DC: Cato Institute.

_____. 1998. "Microsoft and the Browser Wars: Fit to be Tied." *Policy Analysis* No. 296. Washington, DC: Cato Institute.

Liebowitz, Stan J. and Stephen E. Margolis. 1999. *Winners, Losers & Microsoft*. Oakland, CA: Independent Institute.

Lavoie, Don. 1985. *National Economic Planning: What is Left?* Washington, DC: Cato Institute.

Litan, Robert E. and William A. Niskanen. 1998. *Going Digital*. Washington, DC: Brookings Institution and Cato Institute.

McChesney, Fred S. and William F. Shughart II, editors. 1995. *The Causes and Consequences of Antitrust: The Public-Choice Perspective*. Chicago, IL: University of Chicago Press.

McKenzie, Richard B. 2000. *Trust on Trial: How the Microsoft Case is Reframing the Rules of Competition*. Cambridge, MA: Perseus Books.

_____. ____. "Microsoft's 'Applications Barrier to Entry': The Missing 70,000 Programs." *Policy Analysis* No. 380. Washington, DC: Cato Institute.

_____. 1988. *The American Job Machine*. New York, NY: Universe Books.

Poole, Robert W. Jr. 1982. *Instead of Regulation: Alternatives to Federal Regulatory Agencies*. Lexington, MA: Lexington Books.

Posner, Richard A. 1999 [1969]. *Natural Monopoly and Its Regulation*. Washington, DC: Cato Institute.

_____. 1976. *Antitrust Law: An Economic Perspective*. Chicago, IL: University of Chicago Press.

Reddy, Bernard J., David S. Evans, and Albert L. Nichols. 1999. *Why Does Microsoft Charge So Little for Windows?* Cambridge, MA: National Economic Research Associates.

Reich, Robert B. 1987. *Tales of a New America*. Washington, DC: Times Books.

Shapiro, Carl and Hal R. Varian. 1999. *Information Rules: A Strategic Guide to the Network Economy*. Boston, MA: Harvard Business School Press.

Smith, Adam. 1981 [1776]. *An Inquiry into the Nature and Causes of the Wealth of Nations*. Indianapolis, IN: Liberty Classics.

Snell, Bradford C. 1974. "American Ground Transportation: A Proposal for Restructuring the Automobile, Truck, Bus and Rail Industries," Appendix A in *Industrial Reorganization Act Hearings on S. 1167*, 93rd Congress.

Sowell, Thomas. 1980. *Knowledge and Decisions*. New York, NY: Basic Books, Inc.

Stigler, George. 1968. *The Organization of Industry*. Homewood, IL: Richard D. Irwin, Inc.

Weaver, R. Kent. 1985. *The Politics of Industrial Change: Railway Policy in North America*. Washington, DC: Brookings Institution.

Wedgwood, Cicely Veronica. 1955. *The Great Rebellion: The King's Peace, 1637-1641*. Volume 1. London, England: Collins.

Wilcox, Clair. 1971. *Public Policies Toward Business*. Homewood, IL: Richard D. Irwin, Inc., fourth edition.

Wilson, James Q. 1989. *Bureaucracy: What Government Agencies Do and Why They Do It*. New York, NY: Basic Books.

Index

About the Author

David B. Kopel joined The Heartland Institute as director of the Center on the Digital Economy in May 1999. He is also an Adjunct Professor of Law at New York University School of Law, Research Director for the Golden, Colorado-based Independence Institute, and an Associate Policy Analyst with the Cato Institute.

Kopel graduated magna cum laude from the University of Michigan Law School, and received a B.A. with Honors in History from Brown University. He served as an Assistant Attorney General for the State of Colorado, representing state agencies in the enforcement of hazardous waste laws, solid waste laws, Superfund, and other environmental laws. He also served as an Assistant District Attorney in New York City.

Kopel has written seven books, dozens of articles in scholarly journals, and hundreds of magazine and newspaper articles. He has appeared on Nightline, McNeil-Lehrer, and many other programs, and has been quoted by *The Wall Street Journal*, *Time*, the *New York Times*, the *Washington Post*, and many other publications. He also presents a weekly commentary on KBDI Channel 12's public affairs program "Colorado Inside-Out."

While best known for his work on the second amendment, Kopel's interests and writings are wide-ranging, and include constitutional law, property rights, environmental regulation, and e-commerce. He has written on the Microsoft antitrust case, encryption, and CALEA (Communications Assistance to Law Enforcement Act). In his capacity as Research Director for a state-level think tank since 1992, he has solicited, edited, and promoted scores of studies on a wide range of public policy issues.

As Director of Heartland's Center on the Digital Economy, Kopel oversees production of policy studies, feature articles, and opinion editorials on issues pertaining to the role and effects of government in the emerging digital economy. He is The Heartland Institute's principal spokesperson on these issues to the media and at events.

About The Heartland Institute

T he Heartland Institute is a tax-exempt, nonprofit research organization devoted to filling the information needs of elected officials, journalists, and the interested public on a wide variety of public policy issues.

Over one hundred academics and professional economics and 130 elected officials participate in Heartland's research program by conducting peer review of works such as this, suggesting topics, and contributing research and commentary. Over 1,000 donors support Heartland's work with charitable contributions.

Since its founding in 1984, The Heartland Institute has published hundreds of commentaries, nearly 100 policy studies, and a dozen books. It also offers electronic clearinhouses of research produced by other think tanks at its Web site, www.heartland.org, as well as by fax-on-demand.

Heartland's work is overseen by a 15-person Board of Directors and implemented by a full-time staff of 13, identified below.